IN GOD'S TRUTH

IN GOD'S TRUTH

by Nick Bunick

Cover design by Marjoram Productions

For information write:

Hampton Roads Publishing Company, Inc.
134 Burgess Lane
Charlottesville, VA 22902

Or call: 804-296-2772
FAX: 804-296-5096
e-mail: hrpc@hrpub.com
Web site: http://www.hrpub.com

If you are unable to order this book from your local
bookseller, you may order directly from the publisher.
Quantity discounts for organizations are available.
Call 1-800-766-8009, toll-free.

Library of Congress Catalog Card Number: 98-73382

ISBN 1-57174-129-1

10 9 8 7 6 5 4 3 2 1

Printed on acid-free recycled paper in Canada

Table of Contents

Preface

An idea of God's cannot be defeated. I discovered this reality several years ago, which placed me on a pathway that I never dreamed I would travel. Since that time I have shared the messages that "spirit" has provided to me with thousands of people in live audiences and millions of people on television and radio. And now I am compelled to continue my journey by having written *In God's Truth*.

And yet I cannot take credit for truly being the author. There were times as I wrote that I knew the words were coming from a source with much greater wisdom and knowledge than I am consciously aware of. You will discover, as I did, the energy, style, and forcefulness of the words changing from chapter to chapter: the gentleness and compassion to be found in the chapter on Death, explaining that there is no such event, but only transition; the wisdom and beauty found in the descriptions of our relationship with God in the chapter entitled God; the thunder and controlled anger in the chapter on Distortions, explaining how the messages of two thousand years ago, of Jeshua (Jesus) and Paul, were changed. Messages of love became messages of fear; messages of compassion became messages of guilt; and the messages that were designed to foster brotherly love and tolerance were, instead, converted to messages that created prejudice and bigotry and polarized our brothers and sisters.

I knew that I was being guided by sources outside of my own consciousness as I wrote *In God's Truth*. But, whether my co-authors were God, Jeshua, my angelic guides, or my own higher self, I was consciously aware that many, many readers would feel the spiritual healing and uplifting of their own souls. I was also aware that others would feel that their belief systems were being challenged.

So, while one part of me anguished, another part of me—that part of me that is the part of God that is inside all of us—cried out with hope and inspiration, "It is time to tell the truth; it is time for people to know the truth, in God's truth." *In God's Truth* offers evidence of the true messages of Jeshua and Paul that were distorted and changed; and how and why new messages were fabricated sixteen hundred years ago. *In God's Truth* will reveal to you that each one of you is on the same journey; you will be given proof that God has given to each of you loving guides who are God's messengers, the angels; you will learn that there is no such thing as death, only continuance and transitions between heaven and earth; you will be given proof that the concept of a supernatural evil force and a place of eternal suffering, hell, are fabrications of the pre-medieval church; you will be given proof that we are all children of God and that Jeshua (Jesus) is the spiritual guide for any of you who choose to have him, regardless of your spiritual beliefs.

I share with you your true relationship with God and that it is not the end of the world that is coming in the new millennium, but instead, the beginning of a new world, a world that will be filled with love and compassion; and together, as children of God, we shall make it on earth as it is in heaven. And I share with you that the billions and billions of dollars that are being spent today on weapons of destruction throughout the world will instead be spent to feed the hungry children of the world, to wipe out disease, and to raise the standard of living for all of God's children throughout the globe.

I know that, together, through the gift of free will that God has given to us, we can make God's will become a reality. For I do know, with all my heart and soul, that an idea of God's cannot be defeated.

God bless you all as you continue on your journey.

Nick Bunick

Acknowledgments

Many people in our lives participate in making our personal journey a successful one. It would be impossible for you, me, or any other person, to acknowledge every individual who is part of our lives, who help us in creating our dreams and then assist in making those dreams a reality; who give us encouragement when we feel down, who give us hope when we cannot see the light, who give us strength when we feel weak, and inspire us to heights of achievement that we do not think we are capable of accomplishing.

I first want to thank the members of my staff, who I consider my mortal angels who work with me on a daily basis. Beth Ayres, Heather St. Clair, Melissa Milligan, and Kim Bunick, thank you for the love and support that you provide me everyday. We could not have accomplished what we have in the last two years, without the commitment and loyalty that you have given me, and the spiritual strength that you continue to share with me.

To my angel ladies, scattered around the United States, who have provided me with personal messages from my angels and yours, and have kept me on the path of my journey, I thank you for sharing with me the wonderful gift that God has given you. Julie Bontier, Atira Hatton, Jacqueline Ellis, Patty Reed, and Echo Bodine, and to the others who help me continue to follow the light and to recognize the pathways that are before me, I am forever grateful. You have used your clairvoyance to help so many others, I know that the angels sing for joy, recognizing you are not misusing the talents and gifts which were uniquely given to you.

To Doreen Virtue, I am always grateful to be in the company of your wonderful energy and to witness the joy and love that you share with all those who come in contact with you. To Almine Barton, your profound wisdom has inspired me on many occasions. Thank you on behalf of all those who benefit from your healings and your gifts.

Thanks to my family, my wife, and my children for their continued support. When I crossed that threshold in sharing with the public my experiences, you were always there showing strength and loyalty, giving me encouragement in what otherwise could have been a very difficult period in my life.

I want to acknowledge the many thousands of people who have written to us, who have shared their own personal experiences, whether they be angelic experiences surrounding 444, or other ways that God has intervened in their lives, thank you, thank you, thank you. You are the reason that *In God's Truth* has been written. By sharing with me how your lives have been touched by *The Messengers*, by our monthly newsletter and by my symposiums, you inspired me to find the time and energy to work with "spirit" to bring you *In God's Truth.*

Lastly, I want to thank my angels for all their love, guidance, and support. I want to acknowledge the role that Jeshua (Jesus) is playing in my life, in being my guide along my spiritual path, and helping me ascend the mountain, on my journey to be closer with God. I want to thank God for giving me the opportunity to participate in this life mission that I have been given.

IN GOD'S TRUTH

Chapter
- 1 -

The Monster Named Fear

When the child was very young, the child was taught that there was a closet in his or her bedroom; and the child was taught that in the closet there was a monster. And the monster's name was Fear.

And the child was warned that the monster should never be let out of the closet. If the child did not obey, surely God would punish the child. And then, when the child's body died, the spirit of the child would be put into a devastating place called hell; the child's spirit would be punished, tortured, and burned for millions of years into eternity.

And the child was warned that, if the monster was let out of the closet, a supernatural evil force would take over the child's mind and soul and require the child to do acts of evil, leading to the child's soul being punished by God by burning in that eternal hell.

And the child was continually taught to believe that there would be people who on occasion would try to persuade the child to open the closet door to let Fear be released and that the child should recognize that these people trying to persuade the child were wicked people who hated God; and the child was taught that God would punish these people, for surely the child would recognize that these people were agents of the supernatural evil force that was an enemy of God.

The lessons were so reinforced in the child, that the monster was not only contained in the bedroom closet, but also in the mind and heart of the child.

As the child grew older, Fear was accepted through continued reinforcement. The child was too young to question and understand what he or she was being taught. The child only knew that somehow he or she would learn how to live with Fear and would always be on the alert to recognize the enemies of God, who might try to persuade the child at various times in life to release the monster.

Was it not the responsibility of these teachers and preachers to give the child the strength and vigor to contain Fear in their hearts and to recognize God's enemies when they would try to persuade the child to live otherwise by releasing the monster Fear?

When the child became an adult, the closet grew larger, the monster grew larger, and the teaching had succeeded. For the child, who was now an adult, had learned to live with Fear. In fact, these lessons that had been learned so well enabled these adults themselves now to become teachers and preachers, teaching their children that this monster also lives in their closets, and that their children should also protect and respect Fear.

On the morning of October 15, 1997, my colleague, Brian Hilliard, and I walked into the aging building of the newspaper publishing house in St. Paul, Minnesota, where the child who was now an adult was waiting for us. He was leaning on the counter as we entered the lobby. He was wearing a gray cardigan sweater, and wire-rimmed glasses were pressed against his silver hair.

As I approached him and shook his hand, I immediately recognized by his body language, his forlorn look, and his animosity, that the child who was now a man had resigned himself to having lived with Fear. And, by his wary looks of suspicion and frustration, he recognized me as the enemy, a person who had rejected Fear, a person who was trying to corrupt the minds of others by trying to persuade them to open their closet doors and throw the monster out of their lives.

We walked up a flight of stairs into a nondescript conference room. The man motioned for Brian and me to sit across from him. He took out a pencil and a pad of paper. He cautiously looked at me over the lenses of his glasses, with his head slightly bent, his face masking a painful scorn, and began the interview.

He was the religion editor of the newspaper. I did not know if he had volunteered, or had been assigned the task of interviewing me. I only knew that he was engulfed in great discomfort and that Fear had been successful in controlling this man's heart and soul for many years. I asked him if he had a tape recorder, so that my remarks and comments could be quoted correctly. He told me it would not be necessary, for he would take careful notes, as his pencil poised above his lined pages.

I knew the questions that he was going to ask, for he was not a stranger to me. I had met him in many other cities across America the previous few months that I had traveled. Sometimes he would wear a tie, sometimes a sweater, sometimes a dress. Sometimes he was tall and thin, other times short and heavy, and even sometimes a pretty lady. No matter what the outside image, I always recognized the child that had grown into an adult. An aura of gloom was worn like an invisible garment around the man. Although it couldn't be seen, it could be sensed, felt; it almost was capable of being touched and tasted. It was the aura of Fear.

He began to ask me the same questions I had heard many times, in the same wary tone, with the same discernible hint of scorn and discontent. He told me he would write his notes as I gave my answers. I placed my chin on my right hand, my elbow resting on the pine-colored wood conference table, and I closed my eyes as I carefully answered his questions.

Brian and I had just flown into the "Twin Cities" on a 6:00 A.M. flight from Cleveland, and the day before had flown into Cleveland on a 6:00 A.M. flight from Memphis. This was the twenty-seventh city of my book tour, and although my commitment to share what I knew to be truth had never waned, I was tired. Surely the man would not object to my resting my head as he took his careful notes.

He asked me why I claimed that the story of the apostle Paul was not accurate. Did it not say in the Bible that Paul was on his way to Damascus from Jerusalem to persecute Jews in Syria when they had accepted Jesus as the Messiah? Did not Jesus then appear before Paul, temporarily blinding him, and did not Paul then make a conversion?

I explained to him that Paul was not in a position to persecute anyone. I asked how it would have been possible for a person of the Jewish faith to travel 140 miles from Jerusalem to the foreign country of Syria, to persecute Syrian citizens because he did not like the way they were practicing their religion? I asked, would it not have the same probability that Iraqis from Baghdad could travel to Minneapolis to persecute Christians because they were not practicing the Islamic religion?

I carefully answered the man's question by explaining that, when Jesus came to Paul in the desert outside the gates of Damascus, Paul did not make a conversion. There was nothing to convert to. It was Paul who founded Christianity several years later. So, how could Paul convert to something that did not yet exist? It was a commitment that Paul had made. Not a conversion. A commitment to spend the rest of his life teaching the messages of God and Jesus. And it was the pre-medieval church, four hundred years later, that insisted on calling Paul's commitment a conversion.

As I carefully answered his questions in a quiet and gentle manner, I had tried not to arouse the monster Fear. But I could feel Brian continually poking me in my ribs with his right elbow. I thought, what do you want, Brian? Surely this man does not take offense to my resting my head on my hand, as he is taking his careful, copious notes.

It was only later, after the interview, that Brian told me that he was poking me because the man had not been taking notes. Instead, he had been staring at me incredulously, as he had tracked from one question to another. His years of training had recognized me for what I was. Was I not the enemy of God he had been warned about as a child? Was I not truly influenced by the supernatural evil force? Was I not speaking words that were attempting to persuade others to open their closet door and remove Fear?

How dare I explain that two thousand years ago there was a dump outside of the city of Jerusalem called Gehenna? And that the people of Jerusalem would bring to Gehenna their refuse, their throwaways, and that the dump burned twenty-four hours a day. And when one person would get mad at another, they would say in jest or in anger, "Go spend the rest of your life burning in Gehenna." How dare I claim that the English translation of Gehenna was "hell" and that Gehenna was the model for the fourth-century church for the creation of the concept of hell.

How dare I attack fear. Where would people's souls go when God punished them, if I were to convince people of my lie? No wonder the man sat engulfed in Fear, unable to write my words with his poised pencil, but instead to stare at me with contempt.

Weeks later I read the following excerpts of his article in his newspaper. He did not share my words of universal love or universal compassion. Instead, he composed his own words of Fear. Some of the excerpts were as follows:

The Messengers Offers Little Help on Spiritual Journey

> . . .Finally, God has allowed us to meet the apostle Paul, and he is one slick and cool hombre. . . . Bunick claims his life has been radically changed by the angelic message that seeps into his brain every day and laps over into flashy books about spiritual messengers. . . . I decided to speak with the fellow during his Twin Cities visit in desperate hope that all is not bogus in the world of today's religion. . . . He informed me that God speaks through him. . . . When I asked Bunick about his own Damascus road experience, he lowered his head, placed his hands at his temples and began to recite, as if in a trance. . . . Bunick says he can slip in and out of the St. Paul personality when he wants. . . . During the hour I spent with Bunick, no sexless, long-haired, 7-foot tall angels appeared. . . . What aura of mysterious gas has dulled our sense, allowing this story to captivate the intellects of thousands—hundreds of thousands—of otherwise sane people? This is not the truth. . . . One truth about truth remains: It is a hard-fought discovery and almost beyond human grasp. Perhaps there is one other: You can't get there from the pages of *The Messengers*.

The man asked me as I was leaving, "Why do you believe we have to come back again? Isn't life miserable enough that we don't have to do it again?" To this day I feel sorry for the man who never learned to release Fear and never learned how to enjoy the journey we are all on.

Several weeks earlier, in the friendly confines of Kansas City, I delivered a 90-minute presentation in the beautiful auditorium of the national headquarters of the Unity Church. It was a mini-version of the three-hour symposium I was presenting across the United States. The event had been billed as an "author appearance," but the approximately two hundred people who came to the presentation knew that my words, instead, would be a sharing of the messages of Jesus and Paul, as I knew them to have been spoken two thousand years ago.

At the completion of my mini-symposium, I allowed time for people to ask questions. As always, a feeling of love and sharing had been created during the presentation that now filled the auditorium hall. I often think of it as the creation of sacred space, for I can feel the energy and love emanating from the hearts and souls of my audience; I can feel the presence of their angels. That day was not an exception.

As I stood on the stage behind the podium of this impressive facility, with a small portable microphone attached to the collar of my shirt, I saw a petite, elderly woman in the rear of the hall raise her hand, and I acknowledged her. She asked in a very quiet and hesitant voice, "Do you believe that Jesus died for our sins?"

I looked across the auditorium at this loving, gray-haired lady with sadness in my heart. I could feel the pain of the burden she had been carrying all these years. Why, God, have they taken this child, who is now a senior adult, and convinced her to carry this guilt all these years of her mortal life?

I slowly and gently responded by asking her, "Are you referring to the sins that you were told you were born with as you entered this world from your mother's womb, or to sins you committed during this lifetime?"

In her hesitation to answer, the entire audience turned their eyes toward her. I could feel them sharing my compassion, wanting to reach out and embrace her with love, to open her door and allow Fear and his companion, Guilt, to be released now and forever.

She momentarily stumbled as she replied, "Well, I guess the sins I committed in this lifetime."

I answered, "What sins could you have committed in this lifetime, two thousand years after our beloved Brother died on the cross, for which you would take the responsibility of his death? If Jeshua (Jesus) was with us today, not only in spirit, which he is, but standing next to me on this stage, he would tell you that he lived for you, not died for you. He died on the cross to show his love for God and his commitment to God's messages. But he lived for us, not died for us. And he would never ask you to carry the burden of that guilt."

I prayed in my heart that she would understand my answer. I prayed, "God, please release her from this burden so she can experience the love of Jeshua (Jesus) in her life without the burden of guilt. Please, God, allow her to release from her fragile shoulders, from her kind heart and loving mind, the incredible burden of the belief that she somehow is responsible for our beloved brother dying on the cross two thousand years ago. Please, God, allow to be erased the feeling of guilt that the teachers and preachers of Fear and Guilt had put upon her, since she was a young and vulnerable child."

Chapter
- 2 -

Crossing the Threshold

There may come a time in your life when you reach a critical point and are faced with a major decision. There will be a threshold in front of you, and you must decide whether or not you are going to cross that threshold or turn your back to it. And in making that decision, once having crossed that threshold, your life will never be the same again. Having crossed that threshold, it will have been a decision of no return.

Come with me to that threshold. Be there with me, for I want you to evaluate in your mind what you would have done, if you had to make the decision whether or not you would have crossed that threshold.

Let us pretend that you are a woman in your early forties. You have two young children who are teenagers in high school. You live in a modest neighborhood in a friendly town; you like your neighbors, and in turn, you have their respect. Your husband is employed in a middle management position for a small local company. You took a job as a bank clerk several years ago to earn additional money for the college education of your children, and because it had been difficult getting ahead on just your husband's income. You grew up in a family that believed in God, and, like your parents before you, your family goes to church occasionally, although you do not think you are overly religious.

One day you receive a phone call from a woman friend who invites you to visit her on Saturday, so that the two of you may spend some time together. She lives on the outskirts of town, a mile or so off the main road, where there are attractive woods and the houses are far apart. When you arrive at her home, there is a note on her door telling you she had to run an errand and that she would be back in an hour. "Make yourself at home." It is a beautiful spring day, so you decide to take a walk along the dirt road next to her home. The road takes you deeper into the quiet woods, further from the main road. As you enjoy your peaceful stroll, you are conscious of the sounds of nature around you; the fresh country air; and the smell of the pine trees, the firs, and the cedars. To your right there is a lovely piece of property with a sign announcing that it is for sale.

Your heart and mind is at ease, and you are grateful to have these quiet moments to yourself. All of a sudden you hear a strange, loud popping noise to your right, the kind of sound you made as a child when you blew up a paper bag with the air from your own breath and then smashed it with both your hands. You are startled, and, as you turn towards the sound, your entire body freezes and your heart begins to pound. Standing in front of you is an angel, a beautiful angel, translucent, bluish and white in color, with wings by its sides.

The angel is smiling at you, and the fear leaves your heart. But you are paralyzed with the awe and excitement of this incredible moment. The thought flashes through your mind for several seconds that you wish somebody was there with you to witness what you are experiencing.

You hear the angel's voice, but you are not consciously aware if it is speaking out loud or if the words are being spoken in your mind. But there is no question or doubt as to what she is telling you. The angel is telling you in a gentle, quiet, loving voice that God wants you to become a messenger to others of God's love, and of the plans God has for the future of mankind. The angel is telling you that God wants you to purchase this property in front of you, and to build a shrine memorializing this experience you are having, that you should leave your job and spend the rest of your life teaching others to have faith in God and to love one another.

You are told that God has given you free will. It is your decision either to accept the responsibility that God is asking you to undertake or to reject it, and instead, continue life as it has been. The angel suddenly begins to grow fainter to your vision, and you now find yourself alone, in this beautiful sacred spot.

What do you do? Do you run home to your husband and share the news? Do you contact the local media and share your experience? Do you leave your job, buy the property, and begin to build a shrine? If you go public with your story, will people believe you? What effect will it have on your husband's job? How will it affect your children and their lives? Will your neighbors become uncomfortable around you? Which friends will support you and which ones will shun you, certain that you have lost your mind?

Would you cross that threshold?

Now, instead, follow me along my own personal path, and pretend that you are in my shoes. You grew up in a poor neighborhood, a short distance outside of a major city on the eastern seaboard. Your father and mother came to this country when they were young children. Your father was a factory worker, and your family never owned a car or a home. Although they were not educated, they were desperately committed to your receiving a college education. But they knew that they did not have the money to pay for that education.

You worked very hard in school, both academically and in athletics, in hopes of being offered a scholarship. In spite of your parents not being educated, they taught you important basic values that became instilled in you and part of you—values such as honesty, trust, generosity, kindness, and compassion. You did not have a formal religion, but you were exposed as a youngster to the teachings of the religions of your friends, and you found them confusing and difficult to understand. But you respected their belief systems, just as you were taught to respect the teachers and the principal in your school, your family doctor, and the policemen who walked the streets.

You learned at a very young age how to survive. You grew up "street smart." You had to, for you had no choice. But you also grew up knowing there was a special place in your heart for God. You also had a special love for Jesus, even though you did not really know who he was. You could not explain it, but you knew it, even as a young child. You were not religious, but you had a one-on-one relationship with God that was spiritual; but you kept it private, to yourself. And your values were very different than many of your friend's values. You would not steal or be destructive of the property of others. But of even more interest, you would not lie, you would not talk badly about others, you very rarely swore, and you felt love and compassion for all your friends.

Both in junior high school and in high school, you had many achievements. You were president of your class and captain of the athletic teams and enjoyed popularity among your classmates. But it actually embarrassed you rather then made you feel arrogant or special. And in school you would often seek out the least popular classmates to be seen with you at recess and in the school cafeteria, because you thought it would help them with their self-esteem and give them confidence to make friends with other schoolmates.

When you graduated from high school, you had offers from a number of different colleges, including several Ivy League schools—schools like Dartmouth and Brown—to accept a football scholarship. But with the wisdom of an eighteen-year-old kid from the ghetto, you chose to accept an athletic scholarship to a university in the deep South, where football was a priority, for you knew that in attending that school you would not be a financial burden to your parents.

Four years later you graduated, occasionally making the dean's list, earning your education through playing football, playing too much on weekdays and not enough on weekends. Upon graduation, you also were awarded a commission as a lieutenant in the army. Because of your academic achievements and having been an athlete, the military provided you special training. One year later you found yourself second in command of seventeen hundred men in a military organization called "Special Troops." When you were released from your military duty, you recognized that you had been exposed to an incredible educational experience. You truly believed in your heart you could be anything in life that you choose to be and could accomplish anything in life that you committed yourself to.

Many years have now gone by. You own several corporations and have become a very high-profile person in the part of the country where you have settled. You live in a beautiful home on a private lake and have four children who are grown now, three who have graduated from college and one who was still in school. You are on the board of directors of several other corporations. Your wife has her own successful professional career, and your reputations are very important to both of you.

Then one day, you found yourself standing at the threshold of no return. God had intervened in your life, intervened in a very major way. From not having believed in angels, you now find yourself having repeated angelic experiences. You even ask them about your spirituality. You tell them that you are not the same spiritual person you had been as a child—that you have now become competitive, materialistic, and driven to success, that you have lost your spirituality. Why did they choose you? They respond that you had to have those experiences, to prepare you for what is ahead of you, and that you had not lost your spirituality. It will come to the surface again. They also tell you an extraordinary fact—that your spirit and soul had lived two thousand years ago and had walked with the Master, Jesus.

They tell you that God wanted you to accept a mission, to teach God's messages and the messages of Jesus for the rest of your life. But that decision was yours, through the free will that God has given to all of us.

Would you cross that threshold? How would it affect your business life? Would you be asked to leave your positions on the boards of directors that you currently enjoyed? Would you become embarrassed and an embarrassment to your children? How would it affect your wife's career? Also, your wife is a Catholic. How would it affect her life, and what would her family, whose opinion was very important to you, think of you? The public and the media had often described you as being creative. Would they now think that you had created a scam? Or would they think you had lost your sanity?

Would you cross that threshold?

On December 1, 1996, our book, *The Messengers*, was released in Seattle and Portland. I had chosen to cross that threshold.

Earlier that year, in the spring of 1996, the angels awakened me at 4:44 in the morning, and I was told that the book would be written and distributed in Seattle. When I went into my office later in the morning, there was a phone message waiting for me on my desk. The message read to call Gary Hardin in Seattle. When I returned the call, Gary, who had shown great interest in my story two years earlier, told me that he was now living in the Seattle area and was working as a freelance writer. He said that he had heard that I had been keeping a journal of incredible spiritual events that had been happening in my life. He asked if I would be willing to let him read the journal. I said yes, and I sent it to him.

A week later Gary called me on the phone and asked me if he could rewrite my journal, in third person, as a book. He promised he would interview in great detail every person involved, and that he would not bastardize the story. He would not make a Hollywood version out of it. He would only write the truth, as I experienced it. He told me it would take him approximately five months to write it, and I said "go for it."

Gary wrote it in five weeks.

When *The Messengers* came to the marketplace in Seattle and Portland on December of 1996, it immediately became the number one best-seller in the Pacific Northwest. Over twenty thousand copies of the paperback book, which we self-published, were sold the first two months.

The first half of the book shared the story of how God had intervened in my life. It told of the psychics and mystics who claimed that my spirit and soul had lived two thousand years ago in the person we know as the apostle Paul. For fourteen years, beginning in 1977, I did not want to acknowledge it or deal with it, even though I had come to accept this information as truth after I had been told by nine different sources in three different states, totally independent of each other, that, indeed, my spirit and soul had lived two thousand years ago as the apostle Paul.

Who was going to believe it?

By 1991, I was no longer the innocent child in a poor "street smart" neighborhood outside of Boston. Even though my "closet" was totally filled with Love, not Fear, I was now a high-profile businessman, who owned several corporations and who sat on the boards of directors of others. I realized that I had achieved what some think of as the American Dream, for they mistakenly assume that wealth creates happiness, which is not true.

I have come to understand the true meaning of happiness. If you were to place a hundred people in a room, all of whom were people of great wealth, and you asked them, "Are you happy?"—and every one of them were required to tell the truth—some would tell you they were happy and some would say they were not. For happiness has nothing to do with wealth.

If you placed a hundred people in a room, all of whom were people possessing great power, and you asked them, "Are you happy?"—and every one of them was required to tell the truth—some would say they were happy and some would say they were not. For happiness has nothing to do with power.

If you placed a hundred people in a room, all of whom were high achievers, and you asked them, "Are you happy?"—and every one of them were required to tell the truth—some would say they were happy, and some would say they were not. For happiness has nothing to do with achievements.

But if you placed a hundred people in a room, all of whom truly understood their relationship with God and were in harmony with that part of God that is inside of them, their own immortal spirit and soul, and you asked them "Are you happy?"—they would all say yes. For it is being in harmony with your own spirit and soul that is part of God that brings you true happiness. You may be wealthy or poor, you may be a person with or without power, or you may be an overachiever or an underachiever. You may be any of these and have or not have happiness in your life. For it is only through your relationship with God and being in harmony with what is inside of you, the spirit that God has shared with you, that you find true happiness.

So it was, in 1991, after four years of constant harassment and persistence by a local gifted psychic, that I finally agreed to allow myself to be regressed to a past lifetime through hypnosis with Julia Ingram, a professional hypnotherapist. Over a period of five months together, I experienced twenty-six hours under hypnosis, all captured on tape. We never had an outline or prewritten format. It was always done totally spontaneously.

And, yes, under hypnosis I did experience the life of the apostle Paul, through the memory of my soul mind. It began with my being a child of nine years old, running through my father's fields chasing sheep, in a region of the world called Celicia, on the outskirts of the city of Tarsus. It ended with my dying in Rome at the age of sixty-two.

Not only did I share, on tape, details of the life of Paul never known before, but also at the age of twenty-one, I, as Paul, met Jeshua (Jesus), who was two and a half years older than Paul. Under hypnosis I described details of the life of Jeshua never known before. And, yes, in a number of places the information I shared did conflict with some of what is found in the Gospels and Scriptures. The tapes were translated into a manuscript and the manuscript was called *He Walked With The Master*.

In the summer of 1994, a number of book companies wanted to publish the manuscript *He Walked With The Master*. At that time, Gary Hardin, the writer who later called me from Seattle in 1996, was a senior editor of one of those companies. But I could not allow the story to be published. Surely no one would believe that my spirit and soul had lived in the person we know as the apostle Paul. My business reputation would be destroyed. My private life and my social life would be ruined. It was not fair to my family. I could not step over that threshold.

Surely people would believe that I had either fabricated the entire story or that I was insane. I did not have the courage to move forward with it. I turned down the publishing houses. I knew, in that summer of 1994, that it was a closed matter, never to be heard again. But I was wrong.

At that time I did not believe in angels. Angels? Surely you are joking. Did they not belong in the same toy box as the

Tooth Fairy or the Easter Bunny? But on January 14, 1995, I found out that I was wrong. On that day, God intervened in my life, and my life was interrupted and changed forever.

A miracle is defined as the intervention of God in your life. I have come to realize that angels are the messengers of God, and that angelic intervention in your life is truly a miracle. On January 14, 1995, I had my first miracle.

The angels shared many things with me on that Saturday afternoon. They told me that not only was my experience true, but that they would bring many people into my life who could authenticate and verify that God was intervening in my life, individuals who would be willing to be witnesses. And through the experiences I was to have, and with the support of the witnesses behind me, hopefully I would have the courage to step forward and share the story that was to become a book, *The Messengers*. They told me that I had free will, which is a gift that God has given to every one of us. It is through my free will that I would decide whether or not I was willing to make the same commitment to God today that Paul had made to God two thousand years ago through Jeshua.

There are many things that they told me on that Saturday afternoon of January 14th.

They also told me the numbers "444" would play a very important part in my life, as well as the lives of others. They said that "444" represented the power of God's love.

I did not understand the significance of the "444" when they first shared it with me. I knew that my high school football number had been 44 and that my college football number had been 44. I knew that the security code in my house at that time was 444 and that the voice mail retrieval numbers both at my office and my home were 4444. But I had assumed that this was because of a preference that I had for the 4s. I did not realize that God had already been intervening in my life, through symbolic messages showing the power of God's love.

That evening I received a phone call from a person whom I had only met once. He is a Canadian who was in Geneva, Switzerland, on business. When he called me on the phone, he told me he absolutely did not know why he had phoned me. He told me he was embarrassed and asked me if I was all right. I answered that I was.

He then proceeded to tell me that he had been fast asleep in Geneva and had been woken from a sound sleep, almost startled. He said he looked at the clock, saw that it was 4:44 in the morning, and felt this tremendous compulsion to call me.

I then asked him if he had read the manuscript of *He Walked With The Master* that I had given him on that evening we had met for business over dinner in Portland. He told me that he had read it three times, that it had changed his life, and that it was now sitting on a small table next to his bed. I then told him God had intervened in my life that same afternoon through God's messengers, the angels.

Two days later I went to my office, and a colleague of mine was standing in the reception area waiting for me. He had five sheets of paper in his hand, and he told me that it was important that we meet. We did meet later in the afternoon. As he sat across from my desk, holding the five sheets of paper, he shared with me that he had been awakened very early that same morning. He told me he had felt compelled to get a pencil and pad of paper and had gone downstairs to his family room and had written down many things on those sheets of paper although he did not understand what they meant. But he said he knew he was supposed to give them to me. And he handed them to me.

As I looked at the first sheet, on the top left hand side of the page he had printed 4:44 A.M. There were many things he had written on those pages that were exactly the same words the angels had spoken to me two days earlier on that Saturday afternoon. In reading his notes, I recognized that the messengers of God were now providing me the witnesses that I was told would be made available to me.

Nick

Woke up at this time
By 4:50. this
compete.

4:44 AM

Pauline LeMaster
or
Paulene Le Master

The number 4 is very
important to you.

TRINITY is confused in BIBLE
OR changed in modern writing

FATHER
SON — HOLY GHOST

leaves out – the future
+
light peoples
+
guardian angels

They ~~[crossed out]~~ complete things.

F
S
HS
A

FATHER
SON
HOLY SPIRIT (IN MAN)
ANGELS or spirit guides

DRAW THIS ON YOUR FORE HEAD? (MAYBE)

symbol = 3rd eye minds eye

or 3 dimensional

THAT'S WHY we don't understand

THIS represents the complete spiritual NETWORK for man to fully Evolve — the spiritual path for spirit guides must exist — "SPIRITUAL DNA" = existence of path for spiritual guide to work — some are blessed with this power! END

I often think back, and I have this vision of angels sitting around a conference table. In their discussion, they ask, "What can we do to get Bunick's attention? Why don't we go to Geneva, Switzerland, wake up the Canadian at 4:44 in the morning, and have him call Nick?"

Not only was it necessary to wake him up exactly at 4:44 in the morning, but they had to make sure that he looked at the clock. And rather than calling his wife in Calgary, Canada, or his mother in Winnipeg, they had to be sure that he called me. And they also had to be certain that he specifically told me that he had been awakened at 4:44 in the morning. If not for the angels making sure that all those things happened, there would be absolutely no significance to his call to me.

The same is true regarding my other friend. The angels had to be sure that they not only woke him up at 4:44 in the morning, but that he also looked at the clock and registered the time. They had to compel him, through their will, to pick up a pencil and paper; they placed their thoughts in his head that he had absolutely no idea about the meaning of; and they had him put them down in his own writing. They also had to compel him to log, on the page, the time that he had been awakened, and to make sure that he gave me those documents. Can there be any question about how much influence angels can have in our lives?

And this began the first of many, many "444" experiences.

After the book became available in Seattle and Portland, we began to receive hundreds of letters a week from others who, after having read *The Messengers*, were now having "444" experiences. But that is another story that I shall share in the next chapter.

Chapter
- 3 -
Symbols and Symposiums

Our book, *The Messengers,* was introduced on December 1, 1996. I immediately began to receive phone calls from the local media. All four of the local televison stations contacted me for interviews, as well as our three local newspapers. I know that some people believed then, and perhaps some still do, that the information that I shared was motivated by my ego. I know that conversations took place behind my back throughout the greater Portland area regarding my sanity, my credibility, and my motives. It was the most difficult experience of my life.

And, although some people may have assumed that it was an act of ego, it was not. It was the most humbling experience I had ever had in my life. Every morning and every evening I prayed to God to give me the courage and confidence to match the commitment I had made. I had realized that I had opened the door and crossed the threshold. I could never return to a normal life. Regardless of the success or the failure of the book, people who knew me would never look upon me the same again. I recognized that it could destroy my business reputation, that I could lose many of my friends, and that I could become ostracized, not only in my business relationships, but also my social relationships.

However, my family and my close friends totally supported me. They knew that I was speaking truth, and, in spite of their own anxieties, they did not waiver in their support of me.

Some of the stories got back to me regarding what people were saying behind my back. And it did hurt. A relative of a friend stated that I had demons in my head and that she would pray for me. Interesting enough, it was she who believed in the devil, hell, and a punishing God. But I was the one with the demons.

When the televison media approached me, I asked them that, even if they chose not to believe my story, they still treat it with respect. And they did. And I was grateful.

Although I had initially prayed for God to give me the courage and confidence to match the commitment that I had made, after several weeks I no longer had to do so. My confidence now matched my commitment, and in so doing it was no longer a question of courage.

I share with you the words that I had written in the last two pages of the first half of *The Messengers*, which today represents my credo, the commitment that I live by. They were words that I had written earlier that year in my handwriting, with my pencil. But they were words that have been given to me by God's messengers, the angels.

> *You must believe in yourself at all times. You must never lose faith that you are capable of doing anything in life that you choose to do. And you must always choose the highest. It is not enough for you to choose that you must achieve excellence. For you must believe in yourself enough to accomplish that which others cannot accomplish.*

To believe in yourself, you must have courage that exceeds the need for the consideration of courage. It must be a natural part of your life that avoids any needs for decision making based on whether you have the courage to do that which you must. This must be a belief beyond personal questioning, beyond personal doubt, to a point when it can no longer be considered courage but rather a way of life. This shall be so, for you will believe in yourself.

You must have character that is beyond criticism and is a permanent part of yourself. It is not imagined or pretended. Every moment of your life must be naturally conducted with pride and dignity that cannot be confused with arrogance, but recognized with respect. Your character must always contain compassion and concern for others. This concern will be genuine, for you will never lose sight of your background in trying to understand those you have difficulty identifying with, for they are the majority of the world and the ones that need help the most. You must believe in yourself so that your character never bends, never compromises, and is consistent.

You must believe in your intellect, that no task is beyond your ability to succeed. Your intellect is a gift that you shall not waste and you shall use it to its greatest capacity. You must have the patience and tolerance to realize that others will not always agree with or understand you. But rather than find fault, you shall try harder to reach them, for it shall become your responsibility to serve them. This is your calling. You cannot question it. You must accept it.

In April of 1997, friends and members of my staff traveled the three-hour drive to Seattle to attend my first symposium. Approximately one thousand people attended. It was a very special event, for it was to become the format for symposiums I would give throughout the country in 1997 and 1998 and eventually in other parts of the world.

Following the presentation, I went into a waiting room outside of the lobby of the auditorium waiting for the audience to leave. After about fifteen minutes, I felt badly that I had not gone into the lobby to mix with the people who had been in the audience. When I entered the lobby, there were still approximately two hundred people standing around. They joined me, sharing words of encouragement, tears of joy, and asked me to write inscriptions in their copies of *The Messengers* that they had brought with them. But what was truly extraordinary was that a number of people told me privately, totally independently of each other, that they had seen an angel standing next to me on the stage. They described exactly the same angel—one that was over seven feet tall, lavender, blue, and whitish in color. An angel that I had never seen.

One of the people in the audience was a tremendously gifted clairvoyant. Her name is Atira Hatton. I had never met her before, but now Atira is an important part of my life. Atira has a gift of being able to see into the spiritual world, and she saw hundreds and hundreds of angels in the auditorium. In an interview with *USA Today*, Atira said she had never seen so many angels gathered in one place in her entire life, and that, when I was doing the spiritual healing with the audience, an angel was standing behind every individual. The angels' hands were on the individuals' shoulders, blessing them during my presentation.

But the phenomena of the seven-foot angel was not confined to Seattle. In every city that I traveled to, I always allowed time after each symposium to talk for a few moments with any of those who chose to and to write an inscription in their book if they asked. After every symposium there were always some individuals who would share with me, with great joy in their hearts, and sometimes with tears in their eyes, that they had seen the seven-foot angel, lavender, blue, and whitish in color, standing next to me at the podium.

In October of 1997, we held a symposium in Scottsdale, Arizona. Again, approximately one thousand people attended. I prayed to God prior to the symposium, if God so chose, to allow the entire audience to see the angel, perhaps even to permit it to be captured on film. The *American Journal* national televison show cameramen were there that evening and filmed the entire three-and-half hour presentation. And I asked God, "If the timing is now right, my dear Lord, allow us to share with everybody the angelic presence that You have given to us, so we all may see and accept."

A different phenomenon took place that evening. During the symposium, my seven-foot spiritual guide was not seen. But a number of different people in the audience said they had seen green balls of energy floating around me as I spoke from the podium. This was told to me by approximately fifteen different individuals who were seated in different locations throughout the audience. And I was told by two individuals, who said they were psychics, that during the twenty-five minutes of spiritual healing, they could see the color green coming out of my mouth as I spoke, which then formed circles of energy around me and floated above me. I have since learned that green represents the color of healing.

I cannot explain this phenomena to you, nor can I predict what is to happen in the future. I do believe, however, that God is going to allow something very significant to happen someday as we continue these events that will provide greater confirmation to people that God is performing miracles in our lives, through the intervention of angels, including "444" experiences and other symbols that God may choose to use. When the time comes when you are a witness to one of these experiences, or you are the recipient of angelic intervention, do not be frightened. Accept it, for it is a gift from God.

The angels had told me that "444" means the power of God's love. I kept a journal of these angelic experiences. Let me share some of those entries. During that time, I was involved in phone conversations with a woman from upstate New York regarding humanitarian projects. She was a trustee of an organization that provided funding for various humanitarian projects.

One day she asked me for more information about who we were, what was our goal, and who were we affiliated with? I reluctantly shared with her that I had written a manuscript, and I told her of some of my experiences. She, in turn, told me of a friend of hers, a young lady in her thirties, who had been diagnosed as having terminal cancer. She asked me if I would pray for her. I told her that I would, but that I first wanted to send her my manuscript, and I wanted her friend also to read the material.

Several days later she called me on the phone. She was crying with joy. She told me that prior to receiving my manuscript she had woken up three nights in a row at 4:44 A.M., thinking she was losing her mind. She had told her husband and her girlfriend she could not account for this strange phenomena of awakening at that unusual hour on three consecutive nights. When she had received my journal and read the second chapter regarding my "444" experiences, she wept with joy. She now realized that her angels had been waking her at 4:44 in the morning in preparation for reading my story. She shared my material with her girlfriend who had cancer, and I talked to both of them on a conference call several times. It was not too long afterwards her friend was told by the doctors that she no longer had cancer. She had been healed. "444," the power of God's love.

In August of 1997, we had contracted with a New York publishing house and they had delivered approximately one hundred and fifty thousand copies of *The Messengers* to bookstores around the country. I was placed on a national tour, one that eventually took me to twenty-seven cities, to promote the book. The authors of *The Messengers* were Julia Ingram and Gary Hardin. Gary had written the first half of the book, which described my twenty years of experiences, and Julia had been responsible for the second half, which included the transcribing of the age regression tapes, which we had called, *He Walked With The Master*. But, as the subject of the book, I had the responsibility to promote it through personal appearances around the country.

I have read the words of the skeptics in articles that were written about my experiences. They claimed that "444" is a figment of our imaginations and a coincidence. They asked, "Do not these people know that '444' appears on the clock twice every day?"

Yes, "444" does appear on the clock twice a day. However, does that explain why I have had many hundreds of people write to me after reading *The Messengers* to tell me they woke up in the morning to find that their clock had stopped during the night at exactly 4:44? Does that explain the experience of my friend, who left on a trip with his family to spend a week at Disney World shortly after I shared my story with him, and who, upon returning home, walked into his kitchen with his wife and found their digital clock blinking 4:44?

Does that explain how Doug Fish, the president of the advertising firm that did our initial promotion, logged us into his company book to find that we were his 444th client, then shortly after, how he was awakened at 4:44 in the morning, and then again shortly after, how he turned on his computer to provide his password and found the numbers "444" in large digital format flashing on his screen?

Does that explain my friend whom I shared my story with, who shortly afterwards was cutting down a maple tree in his yard when it began to fall on him? He was convinced that he was going to be killed, but instead found himself being rushed to a hospital in an ambulance. It was a miracle he had not been killed; instead, he had been admitted to the hospital at exactly 4:44 in the afternoon and was then assigned to room 444 in the hospital.

And does it explain the hundreds of letters that we receive from people who have told us that, after they have read *The Messengers*, their security alarm or fire alarm went off at 4:44 in the morning for no apparent reason?

Does it explain about Bobbi Rosenstein of Mount Vernon, Washington, who was visiting her aunt in Chicago who had terminal cancer? Does it explain how, after having read *The Messengers* with her aunt from cover to cover, Bobbi was woken up in the middle of the night after her aunt's spirit had left her body, how a suitcase that had been sitting on a table all day fell to the floor, and how, when she looked at the clock that was sitting on her night stand, it was 4:44 in the morning?

Some individuals who had never allowed the monster Fear out of their closets are skeptics and cynics. They are convinced that the "444" experiences are not coming from the messengers of God, but instead it is the devil, playing games with people's minds. In fact, I have often been asked by them, "How do you know that it is God's angels that are intervening in your life? How do you know that it is not the devil?"

And I always respond that, if it is the devil, he sure has had one hell of a conversion, for he is now asking me to teach others how to embrace universal love and universal compassion and to live in truth. That answer always brings discomfort and fear to them, for they are then able to see the door to their "closet" slightly being cracked open.

And since *The Messengers* was brought to the public nationwide, we have begun to receive hundreds of letters every week. Allow me to share with you some of the interesting stories of those who have had "444" experiences.

Aaron, September 9, 1997

A few weeks ago I was at work and I was having some trouble with my computer. It was after 5:00 P.M. and I was running some diagnostic programs to figure out what the problem was. It was getting kind of late and I wanted to go home. I switched off the computer monitor and figured I'd let the computer run through the program and would be done when I came in the next morning.

The next morning I came in at 8:00 A.M. and turned my computer screen back on and my computer was frozen up and would not respond. It didn't take me very long before I noticed that the computer clock had stopped at 4:44 P.M.! This was very shocking because I had left work well after 5:00 P.M. the day before!

I continue to see "444" everywhere I go, but this experience was the most shocking.

Barrett, September 17, 1997

*It has been an amazing set of "444" experiences for me, and for those who I have recommended the book (*The Messengers*).*

First, I had just finished the book, and told someone about it, and said to her, "Hey, let's see if there is any info on the Internet." So, we started looking at the possibilities, and, as soon as we landed on the site, the page changed right away, and I said, "Look at your computer clock, it is 4:44 P.M. Welcome to the club." Well, after this first experience I recommended the book to a friend and told her just a little bit about it. The day she received it, she dove right in, and the next morning when she opened her store the very first sale of the day rang up to $4.44 and, oh yes, there are many others now, but the one I am more excited about is just last night.

I am a VERY heavy sleeper, and nothing ever wakes me up fully, but I decided I would set my wristwatch to 4:44 A.M. just in case I happen to be awake I would hear it. Well, last night I set the watch for the first time, and I woke up and heard a very light distant thunder and thought to myself that it sounded somehow very peaceful, and, just as I came to full consciousness, my watch began to beep. It was 4:44 A.M. The angels continue to let me know that they are there, and I feel so good to have them with me.

Many people have contacted us to tell us about "444" experiences that have happened in relation to fire alarms. In a restaurant recently, a gentleman and his wife approached me and introduced themselves. He told me that he was an attorney, and that he had read the book while he and his wife were on a vacation in Palm Desert. When he completed the book, they proceeded to go to bed. In the middle of the night the fire alarm went off exactly at 4:44 A.M. in the condominium they were renting. He immediately accused his wife of setting off the alarm to play a joke on him. He then realized that she had been fast asleep herself when the alarm went off and that he had not yet told her about the "444" phenomenon.

Robyn, May 24, 1997

I actually have had two "444" happenings. The first was when I was reading The Messengers *and was awakened at 4:44 A.M. with all the smoke alarms in the house blaring—FOR NO APPARENT REASON.*

Robyn proceeded in explaining another "444" experience that she had had.

Read the book, loved it!! Asked for a sign. The next day I was calling for an address to mail a letter; guess what?—4444. I ordered your newsletter, can't wait. Thank you for bringing so much hope to the millions who will read your book!

Roger, November 3, 1997

Nick, I thank God daily for you and your book, The Messengers. *I've enjoyed reading it and it has helped to answer questions I have had for many years.*

My wife and I drive a truck for a living. We had been talking about your book for some time, on our way to California. When my wife decided to go to bed, when she entered the sleeper, the clock was flashing 4:44.

Kathy, August 25, 1997

The evening after I finished the book I was driving to work and I said, "If I have any angels with me, please communicate with me some way so that I know for sure." When I arrived, there was a new person sitting at my desk, so I took my work into the lunchroom. I was alone when all of a sudden the microwave beeped twice. No one was using it. I looked up and the time was 4:44. I had a huge grin on my face and was staring at the oven when a coworker came in to ask me a question. She looked at the oven and then at me—I know she thinks I lost it, but I was so happy!

Claudia, August 21, 1997

*I became a member of the 444 club two weeks ago, and since then I have experienced this amazing thing two more times. The first time I read a review on the book (*The Messengers*) in my local paper, I did not think much about it till one week later. I had a vivid dream that I was in the middle of a horrible earthquake. I was unable to find my way back home. I was concerned for my son and my mother's safety. I finally* *gave up and sat on the street curb and lowered my head to cry. Then I heard someone call my name several times. When I looked up to see who was calling my name, I woke up and sure enough the clock read 4:44 A.M.*

Mark, September 9, 1997

*My brother Joel recommended the book and told me of his "444" experience. I was doubtful of his story, until I had my own the night after I finished the book (*The Messengers*). I was sound asleep and I awoke suddenly from a large bump sound. I got up and noticed the bedside clock read 4:44. The next day I watched a video called "A Family Thing" and noticed that when Robert Duvall gets out of bed, the clock reads 4:44. In the movie there are two scenes with statues of angels as they drive out of town. I recommend that people ask their angels for a sign. You might be surprised.*

Pamela, September 16, 1997

I had been reading The Messengers *that night. I woke up and I thought I had better go to the bathroom. When I returned I decided to look at the digital clock to see what time it was. To my amazement, the clock said 4:44, not 4:43, not 4:45. A sense of joy and excitement came over me, and I couldn't wait to share with my roommate the next morning. I was also typing an e-mail message to some friends of mine, to whom I plan to tell my story at a future date, and when I looked at the first set of e-mail numbers the first group of numbers were 444!!! Not only that, but my roommate (who would tell her own story) also had a "444" experience after she had read the whole book!!! It's just amazing!!*

Audra, August 12, 1997

*Yes, I know I wrote you earlier, but something else happened today, another "444" incident. I have always had a strange connection with my cousin, that I would have the urge to call her. She would generally reply that she had been thinking about me—so I have gotten to the point where I can just say "what is it" instead of hello. I had that urge tonight, and told her about a book (*The Messengers*) I just finished reading and about the 444s. She said, "Would you laugh if I told you for the last four nights that I have woken up at 4:44 A.M.! It also happens that I had been reading the book for the last four days!!!"*

Emanuele, April 10, 1998

First of all, I would like to say I enjoyed your book tremendously! I have just finished reading it for the second time. It is very uplifting and heartwarming.

A friend of mine had bought the book for me in July of '97. I have read quite a few Angel books since my sixteen-year-old son was shot and killed on September 15, 1996.

I am quite sure I had a "444" experience right after I had read your book the first time. I had just finished reading your book and had gone to the grocery store. As I pulled out of the grocery store parking lot, a van pulled out ahead of me. I looked at the license plate and it read, AMA-444. My son's name who was killed is Anthony Mario Arruda; his initials being AMA. So, when I saw the license plate, I was shocked, seeing how I had just finished reading your book that morning. I know in my heart that it was no coincidence, because God is no coincidence.

God bless you and your wonderful story.

Thank you to all those who have shared your "444" experiences with us. You have been an inspiration for many people. For those who have not had a "444" experience, it is important that you realize that there are many different ways that your angels can be in contact with you. Do not be upset or feel that you are being ignored. It is no different than your having a friend, who with all her heart and soul loves you 100 percent, even though you and she may not knowingly have been in communication with each other. As I will share with you in another chapter, there are many ways that you can open a channel with your angels in addition to their showing you their presence by using symbols.

I had first assumed that "444" experiences were a new symbol the angels were using exclusively for me, and that it had just begun as I became aware of the angelic umbrella I had opened. And I had assumed that others began to have "444" experiences only after having read *The Messengers*, for they then also came underneath our angelic umbrella. While I do believe this is true in most cases, I found out it is not totally accurate. We now receive letters monthly from hundreds of people who had "444" experiences at different times in their lives prior to *The Messengers* having been written.

James Twyman is the author of a wonderful book, *Emissary of Light*. Jimmy and I were both speaking at a spiritual expo in Spokane, Washington, in May of 1998. On the morning of our talks, five of us were having breakfast together, including Nancy Walsch, the wife of Neale Donald Walsch, the author of *Conversations With God*.

During breakfast, Jimmy told us a wonderful "444" story. One month earlier, on April 23, he had participated in a prayer vigil at the United Nations building in New York City, which also included playing his music as part of the ceremonies. He was approached by a woman, who told him that four years earlier a Native American shaman had instructed her that she should travel to New York to the United Nations building to attend a very special function that was going to help promote peace in the world. He told her that this function would take place four years, four months, and four days from the day in which he was giving her that instruction, which was the exact day she approached Jimmy.

Following our breakfast, I joined a group at another table to visit with some people who had come to hear my lecture, and the other four who I had had breakfast with walked to the cash register to pay our breakfast bill. I soon heard a commotion and shouts of joy. I looked up to see Nancy Walsch wearing a big smile and with her thumb up in the air. Jimmy ran back to the table where I was seated to tell me that the change from the bill for the five of us had amounted to $4.44. The power of God's love.

In the same year of 1998, a wonderful new Hollywood movie was brought to the public called "The City of Angels." In the opening scene, Nicholas Cage and another angel are having a conversation on top of a high-rise office building in Los Angeles. When the camera panned away from the building, it showed that the address was 444.

Also, one of the main characters of the movie, Dennis Frantz, decided to convert from the angelic realm to become a human. He selected the name of Mr. Messenger. I am sure that our book did not influence these Hollywood screenwriters, for the movie was probably being written at the same time our book was also being written. At the same time God was intervening in our lives with angelic symbols, this was also happening in Hollywood. The power of God's love.

Lastly, last year one of my colleagues was watching the Discovery Channel on television. The moderator was telling of an incident that happened in Egypt in the 1970s. He shared with his audience that the image of the Madonna had appeared above a mosque in Cairo, Egypt, and had been seen by thousands of people. He then showed a copy of the newspaper printed at the time it happened. The date on the newspaper showed that the miracle had taken place on April 4, at 4:44 in the afternoon. The power of God's love.

Chapter
- 4 -
The Angels

Prior to January 14, 1995, I did not believe in angels—perhaps, like many of you. Were they not the myths of poets and tellers of fairytales? In every story I had previously heard of an angel, there was no witness to the angelic event. The acceptance of the story as truth was based on the listener's own level of faith in its truth.

The person who told the story never provided confirmation by others. Was the story of the angel really true? Or was it the fabrication of the individual? Or perhaps their imagination? I did not know, but in the absence of evidence, I had never accepted the possibility of angels being a reality.

But now I have found truth. The word angels comes from the ancient Aramaic word meaning messengers. The angels are truly the messengers of God. They are a precious gift that God has given to each and every one of us. Every one of you have had at least one angel in your life, if not more, from the day you are born. That angel is your guardian, to provide you inspiration during times of despair, hope in times of sadness, courage in times of fear. Most often we are not even aware that angels exist in our lives, but they do.

My understanding and acceptance of God's messengers, the angels, began the first time they intervened in my life—on January 14, 1995. As I think back today, I am not sure how to describe what I was experiencing when I realized that the angels were communicating with me.

Perhaps the best way I can describe what I was feeling is to say that I was in awe. I do remember one moment saying, "I am so blessed, for God is talking to me." And they corrected me and said, "Not God. His guides."

I have now had over fifty angelic experiences. They come in many different forms, ranging from signs such as the "444," by celestial voice, and by claircognizance. They also communicate with me during meditation, during prayers, during my dreams, during my writings, and through others who are clairvoyant, who share their words with me.

To those who doubt the existence of angels, it is possible you may never accept their presence until your spirit leaves your body and you yourself are in the spiritual world. But they are truly just as much a part of your life as they are mine. Of course it is possible that there is another species in the world, other than those that you know. Is it not true that human beings are only one of thousands of species that exist on our planet? Do you not believe that there is a spiritual world, in which spirits do exist? It is most likely that you do believe in a spiritual world, or you probably would not be reading this book. So, surely it should not be difficult for you to accept that there is a species that exists in the spiritual world, a species that is assigned to you. If you choose to call angels by another name, it does not change the substance of what they are: spiritual guides, spiritual companions, angels, or messengers of God, they are with you always.

At different times in your life, different angels are assigned to you to help you perform certain tasks. When you have certain needs beyond your usual needs, other angels are assigned to you to assist you during those times. The angels have told me often that many new angels have come into my life to help me fulfill the mission that I am on. I ask them how that could be. Are not all angels of the same qualities and skills? And their response was, "Why would God waste a highly trained angel on a couch potato?"

Just as a fourth-grade student has a fourth-grade teacher, not a college professor, by the same token, a college student would not have a second-grade teacher, but instead, one who is trained and skilled to teach at the college level. The same is true with our angels. You are assigned an angel consistent with what you are doing in your life at any given time. It does not mean, though, that if you are a couch potato, your angel loves you any less or is any less loving. You very well could have the most loving couch potato angel in the universe. It is not discrimination, but rather an assignment of an angel that meets your needs, based upon those needs at that given time.

I am often asked if angels are able to take human form? I have not experienced an angel in human form that I am aware of. Obviously, we have all heard stories of how a person was helped during an incredible moment of danger or need and that the person providing the help usually came out of absolutely nowhere and then immediately disappeared into thin air following the event. We are then led to believe that the person who provided the help, in reality, was an angel disguised in human form. Again, I have no personal knowledge of such an event, for I have not met, to my knowledge, an angel in a human body. But God does perform miracles.

An angel normally does not have a corporeal body, but instead is translucent. By that, I mean if you have seen an angel, you literally would be able to see through the angel, just as if you held a flimsy nightgown in front of a flood light. Even though you could see the gown, you could also see what was behind the gown in the background.

Also, you cannot tell the gender of an angel, whether they are male or female. Although I am told they do have a gender, you cannot tell if you are looking at a beautiful young woman or a beautiful young man. And, yes, they do have wings.

Some people who are clairvoyant have told me they have seen some angels that were extremely tall, some over seven-feet or ten-feet in height. I have been told this by several different individuals who have clairvoyance, and who I know speak in truth. So I do accept, based on their description, that angels do come in various heights. I do not know if they eat, procreate, sleep, or age. I only know that they do exist and they are a gift to you from God.

How do you come into contact with your angels? If you are not clairvoyant and are not able to see into the spiritual world, and not clairaudiant—not able to hear the spiritual world—and not claircognizant—not able to think or receive information from the spiritual world—there is one other medium I can share with you that I know does work, and one that I use often. It is creating the ability to open up a channel for your angels to be able to write messages to you, using your pencil, your hand, and your penmanship.

If you choose to, you may start an angel journal in which you write letters or messages to your spirit guides. Ask them to join you in sharing their words with you and offer yourself as the medium to reach you. You may start your letter the same each time, such as "Dear God, my Beloved Father/Mother, Dear Jeshua (for those of you who accept Jeshua as your spiritual guide), and my loving angels, please come and join me. Share your thoughts and words with me. I am opening up my heart and soul to allow you to use my penmanship, and my hands, and my pen as your instruments, so you may share information with me."

You then continue along this line. There will come a time you will find yourself writing words and thoughts that are not your creations. The very first time this happened to me,

I remember having sat down with pencil in hand and having asked the angels to come and join me. I was totally convinced that I had written nothing. But the next morning I woke up and went over to retrieve the piece of paper that was sitting on the table in my bedroom by the window. I found the words written in my handwriting, "The rain cannot distinguish need. It falls both in the ocean and in the valley."

I thought of these words many times, for what had been written had a number of different important meanings. I believe that what they were telling me is that there are many times in life that we ask for things, even though they are not needed in our lives, for they do not bring us happiness or joy. "The rain cannot distinguish need. It falls both in the ocean and in the valley."

In September of 1979 I lived through one of the most difficult periods of my life. I went through a separation and a divorce that also involved my leaving the home in which I had been raising my four children whom I loved with all my heart and soul. My family was then, and are today, the most important people in my life, along with my relationship with God. I remember the first couple of weeks of being separated from them. I experienced the greatest pain and sorrow. I remember sitting down one day and asking God and my spiritual guides for advice, convinced again that I had written nothing.

One year later I was moving from that first apartment to another, and was looking through my dresser drawers to pack my belongings into suitcases. It was then that I came across papers that were written in my handwriting and that were dated September 1979, twelve months earlier, the month that I was first separated from my family. And these are the words that I had found written on these papers, in my handwriting, that I was not aware had been written. They were words that came from my spiritual guides.

There are many things that we devote our attention to in life that are meaningless, that do not warrant our energies that we expend; the worry, the time, the loss of happiness. We must control our energies and center them on things we know will bring happiness and peace of mind. We are mind, and in being mind we should not feed our mind garbage or negative thoughts (harmful things), anymore then we would feed our bodies garbage or harmful things.

Control what goes into your mind. Happy thoughts produce happiness. Sad thoughts produce sadness. An onion seed produces an onion. Love is the greatest elixir of all. It cleanses our soul, erases negative feelings, makes us tolerant, patient, caring, interesting, enthusiastic. It can only bring good results and override any other thoughts and emotions that could be harmful.

Do you have any advice for me? I ask you please to come visit with me.

Yes, you need to control your thoughts. You're trying to hurt yourself. Flow with the tide. Accept and do not try to make negative things become unnecessary realities. You have a wonderful capacity for happiness through your intellect and your physical being, your sense of awareness and ability to have others look toward you for leadership. Be love and gentleness, and all around you, shall you create the same. Your understanding is important, in that you know you control your own realities. Therefore, control it for that which can bring you happiness.

Remember, enjoy life every moment. Let others enjoy life through you. Pride and dignity are as natural to you as a swan is to water. But enjoy. It is as you want it to be.

You have a need to punish yourself, because you feel guilt. Do away with it. Reliving the past is negative.

Live now. Now is the most important moment in your life. And now is always now. There is not one moment of your past or any being's past that can compare with the importance of their now. The nows affect and create the realities of the future nows. But there is no more important moment in your life than the now. Live it. Enjoy it. Cherish it. It is God's gift.

You are good internally and you do not have the right to punish yourself, thinking of things that are not, may or may not be; not for pity but for punishment. Enough. I shall give you a key. It shall be yours to always bring you back to love, when you stray. It shall be a thought process that shall always be at your fingertips, whenever you want, always there.

Visualize, either in front of you or in your mind, the letters L. O. V. E. They appear as an object, the four letters as you see them. They are white and flimsy, almost transparent. They now bond into a light cloud of energy, and this cloud now enters your body through the heart and gently expands into all of your being, your spirit, your mind, and you experience vibrations and a slight smile.

It is on your face and in your eyes and you feel and generate love. And it shall come to be that even the slightest smile on your face shall trigger the process of love and also the look of your love in your eyes. A gentle touch, and pleasant sound, a kind voice, "a person in need of love," they and any of them shall become a catalyst of others feeling your love and your being until you and it become one, forever, for always. It is your key to happiness, no matter what happens around you. Wear it always. Never remove it. Be at one with it.

You may call me as often as you wish, more often than you have. This writing is important to you. Let it be regular. With love, I say goodbye for now. But I am always with you.

I have read these words hundreds and hundreds of times over the years. I have a copy on my desk, a copy in my briefcase, a copy on the night table by my bedside. It was my first, real message of substance that I received from my spiritual guides. But there have been many since then.

You also have the ability to open up the channel. It is like having a radio that is in front of you that is off. You must reach over, press the button that says "on". Then turn the knob to find the station in order to receive transmission. There may be static in the beginning; there may be such a faint sound that you are almost inclined to believe that you have not found the channel, but keep trying. I promise you, you will find the channel, for it is there. I know, even as I write these words to you in *In God's Truth*, there are times when the words you will be reading are words that I have created. Other times they will be the words that will be coming from "spirit". At times you will not recognize the difference. And other times it will be very obvious to you.

You must remember that God does not discriminate. I do not care if you are rich or poor. I do not care if you are "new age," religious, or agnostic. You are a child of God, and your Father/Mother will never forget you. Each and every one of you have one or more angels that are in your lives. Accept this gift from God, and let your angels know that you love your spiritual guides. Open your eyes and you shall see; open your ears and you shall hear; open your mind and you shall learn, for God and God's messengers love you.

I will share with you a poem the messengers wrote to me, in my handwriting, on my paper, with my pen. I do not even know the date it was written. I only know it was in my handwriting and was written by "spirit" for you. It was named "Journey of Life."

Journey of Life

Our journey began many years ago
We traveled a great distance from the start.
We climbed over mountains, thru valleys and fields
At times would have quit, had we a fainter heart.

It began with our young faces shining and bright,
Teachers, working hard among our class.
Books and pencils and papers were our tools,
Great efforts were made towards each lad and lass.

The seasons came fast and sometimes slow.
There were moments that were sad and moments of fun.
Winter brought cold and mounds of snow
But was always followed by warmth and sun.

Friends were made, we knew for life
Companions we would never forget.
Our lives were full of so much joy
To our young world, we had little debt.

Then it was time to move along
To compete we must educate.
And the clock of life did not stand still
Step by step, we rose to graduate.

New faces, new names, more demands were made
And hours of study grew longer.
New foods, new clothes, new songs were played
And our bodies grew older and stronger.

We cheered for our colors and sang foolish songs
And thought that ours was the best.
We worked so hard to become so smart
To distinguish ourselves from the rest.

The important day came, no longer a youth,
We dressed alike in robes of black.

IN GOD'S TRUTH

They told us we were now adults
Full speed ahead, no time to look back.

We scrambled around, new towns and streets
We knocked on doors to find our place.
It was a new beginning, one more time
And we were caught in the middle of the race.

Two or three times we changed jobs
Till we found what we knew was right.
Now our energies could be devoted
To reaching our furthest height.

We sought a friend and chose our mate
We created home and the young ones came.
We couldn't understand where the dollar went
As we strove for our fortune and fame.

We clawed and pulled and pushed and shoved
Was not life's object "get ahead?"
Nothing was of more importance
What other path was there to tread?

The home grew larger, the closets fuller
The lawns were green, the cars were sleek.
The prizes were great, accounts were bigger
We could not have done it, had we been meek.

But one day did arrive not too long ago
When the mirror showed us truth.
The years had gone by so fast
What happened to our youth?

The old friends we had made for life
We could not remember their names.
The silly songs, the parties and heros we cheered
We couldn't even remember the games.

The Angels

We think of thoughts not thought before
And of the purpose of the race we ran.
Of the mountain we hiked and climbed
And of the ocean that we swam.

We ask questions of ourselves we had never asked
We wonder if it is too late.
Had we followed the same path as the others
But should some other road have been our fate?

Learning and knowledge did not make us smart
Our slower step finally made us look back.
Was the prize really worth the running
Or had we raced on the wrong track?

But as long as our spirit on this journey does travel
We can still choose to finish it right.
For it is more important to climb the right mountain
For at the top of that peak is a spectacular sight.

We should not care how many years it will take
For the path is covered with warmth and love.
We should not care if time allows us to reach the top
As long as we continue to climb above.

For joy and bliss is for everybody
The rich, and the poor, the young and the old.
Let us not tarry any longer, come join us
If you also are racing on the wrong road.

Chapter

- 5 -

Mystics and Psychics

Prior to January 14, 1977, I did not believe in psychics. I had a vision of psychics being individuals with turbans wrapped around their heads and looking into a crystal ball. I did not realize that the authentic and legitimate psychics of today were the prophets of thousands of years ago.

In the old testament of our Bible there are stories of some of the greatest prophets of history. Many sections of the Bible were written by these prophets. I speak of Daniel, Elijah, Ezekiel, and Malachi as well as many others.

Were not these people of centuries ago revered, respected, and loved by the people, for certainly God had given them a special gift? Were they not able to tell not only what had happened in the past and what was occurring currently, but also what was to happen in the future? Their words of wisdom were called prophecies, and they were called prophets.

Today's legitimate psychics are the prophets of "yesteryear." They can tell you what has happened in your past, what is happening now, and what is to happen in your future. They are not meant to be worshiped or prayed to, for they are not part of the spiritual realm. But they do have a special gift, just as a person may have exceptional talent as a writer, or as a singer, or dancer. Their gift is as natural to them as are the gifts of the artists that we honor in other fields.

Sometimes these gifts come to them after a major accident, or after a near-death experience, or a close-to-death sickness, or some other event of an extraordinary nature that triggered the opening of that channel into the spiritual world. Others are born with it.

At one time or another, I would ask these psychics or mystics: Where do you get your information? Almost without exception, the answer was always, "I don't know." I have now come to understand how psychics and mystics do get their information. I believe they get it from our angels, who, in turn, through claircognizance, transfer that information directly into the minds of the psychics. Although I do not consider myself psychic, this has happened to me several times. I would receive information about another person, which I knew was coming from claircognizance, from the spiritual world.

So, when the psychics and mystics tell you what has happened in your past and in your future, I am convinced they are getting this information from our angels. For I have this vision of our angels standing on top of a mountain and we are directly underneath them. They can look behind us and see where we have been. They can look directly down below and see where we currently are. And they can look in front of us and see where we are going.

However, there are times you will be told about your future, and it will not come to pass. And you may ask, did I receive the wrong information? Is it possible that the psychic or mystic does not truly have the gift of receiving data? Is there such a thing as fate and predetermination?

What about those times when the psychic told us what is going to happen in the future, and it does happen? Or those times the psychic told us of events that are going to happen in the future, and they do not happen?

I am convinced that the reason some events in the future do not happen is because we are given the gift from God of free will. We are the only species in the world that has that gift. God gave us the ability to make decisions for ourselves, as opposed to our being instinctively programmed, biochemically programmed, or programmed through our DNA, to always make the same decisions in similar situations. There are many years in our lives that we walk down a path and there are no crossroads. The path is straight and narrow. Our lives are predetermined in that there are no major decisions that we have to make. And we exercise our free will day after day, regarding the small decisions, that take us into our future.

But every so often our path leads us to a major crossroad, and we then exercise the gift from God of free will. We may choose to take a different crossroad than our angels anticipated we would take. And this is why sometimes we are told of events that will happen in our future but that ultimately do not happen.

It is obvious to me when I came to my first crossroad. In all my early years up to high school there were no major decisions for me to make. There were no decisions by my parents that could have altered my life. My father worked in a factory. We did not own a home or an automobile. It was not possible that we would move to another part of the country. It was never an issue. So, for the first eighteen years of my life the angels could very easily have told a mystic of the events that were going to happen in my life, and they would have come to pass.

But after graduating from high school, as a result of my receiving good grades in school as well as being an athlete, I was offered scholarships to a number of different colleges. I had come to a crossroad in my life. What school was I going to choose? Was I going to go to Dartmouth, Brown, Harvard, Boston University?

I chose to go to the University of Florida on a football scholarship. In so doing, the events that were to unfold in my life were entirely different than if I had decided to go to a local college in the New England area instead. That decision, at that crossroad in my life, to go to college in the deep South, determined the friends I would make over the next few years, where I was to be stationed when I entered the military as a lieutenant through ROTC, the person I wedded in my first marriage, the children we brought into this world, as well as many other future events.

The decision I made at that first crossroad affected my life thereafter, as opposed to my having chosen a different path at that crossroad. I am sure that you can also recognize the different times in your life when you came to a major crossroad and you exercised the gift that God gave you, your free will, and selected a path that you then have stayed on for many years, until you came to your next crossroad.

The simpler the decisions that are ahead of you, the fewer crossroads you come to or the more obvious the path that you will choose upon reaching that crossroad. Then the psychics will be able to share with you what the future holds for you with more accuracy. For then the angels can look down from the top of the mountain and see what is ahead of you and also share with greater accuracy which road you shall select.

Some individuals who have this gift do not call themselves psychics; they call themselves clairvoyant. Unlike the psychics who say to you that they do not know how they get their information, the clairvoyant instead will tell you they are receiving information from your angels. The difference between the clairvoyant and the psychic is that the clairvoyant is getting information either visually, seeing symbols given to them by the angels, or by clairaudiance, hearing the words from the angels. But the psychic receives information through claircognizance, by having it placed into their minds, such as if they are reading a spiritual fax they have just received.

There are more clairvoyants living today than in any other time in history. This is not an accident. It is because of the spiritual consciousness that is spreading throughout the entire world, like never before in the history of mankind.

I feel very blessed that I have become close friends with several extraordinary clairvoyants, and they constantly share their gifts with me. I want to share a story with you that happened to my next door neighbor, so you will understand the significance of the information that clairvoyants can share with you.

Two doors from me lived a person with whom I developed a very close friendship. His name is Dick Benson. Dick had been a senior vice president of a Japanese electronic firm that had a very large plant facility in the Portland area. In spite of his talent, he had been let go because the company chose to put an individual in his position who was trained in Japan. During his job search, I shared with him my experiences regarding the information I received from my clairvoyant friend, and he asked me for her name and phone number. This is what transpired.

Although he had shared nothing with her, she told him, during an angelic reading over the phone, that he would be going to the Rocky Mountain area to run a privately owned company. She told him that the corporation was owned by a man who was in poor health and that the man was small in stature, had blue sparkling eyes, and was like a miniature Santa Claus, having white hair and white moustache. She said that the angels had told her that there were three children, two sons and a daughter, who were employed with the company and that the company had a serious problem with a firm from the state of New York. She told Dick that he would interview for and accept the job, become president of the company, and have a tremendously successful experience with them.

Several days later Dick flew to the Denver airport, and when he arrived there he was greeted by a man who identified himself as the son of the owner of the company. When Dick asked if there were any other brothers or sisters working for the company, he responded yes, both a sister and a brother, who were also vice presidents of the firm. As they were driving to the facility, Dick asked him if they had any special problems. He responded that they had a seven-million-dollar law suit that had been filed against them by a company out of New York.

When they arrived at the facility, Dick was taken to the father's office to meet him. He was exactly as my clairvoyant friend had described. He had sparkling blue eyes, white hair, and a white moustache, and, although he was thinner than the traditional concept of Santa, he did look like a miniature Santa Claus. When they left the office of the father, Dick asked the son about the father's health. The son responded that the father was in excellent health, and Dick thought, "Uh-oh, the angels missed on that one." However, when they returned to the father's office after a tour of the plant, the father's face was ash white. He told his son that he was feeling tremendously ill and asked to be taken to the hospital. At the hospital he was diagnosed, in addition to other problems, as having incredibly high blood pressure and was told by his doctors that he should not return to work. There were many more details regarding the company and the family that the angels communicated to Dick, all of which came to pass.

Dick did become president of the company and did experience tremendous success. Not only did he substantially increase the earnings and profits of the corporation, but they sold the corporation to another firm two years later, as the angels had said, at an increased value that had more than doubled during his presidency. Everything he had been told by my clairvoyant friend through the angels had become a reality.

The phenomena that is now happening to me is that there are a number of people around the country, some who

I have never personally met, who are receiving angelic readings for me. Although they were reluctant at first, they now write me letters and say "Nick, this is what I am being told by the angels and that I am being instructed to share with you." The reason I know the information is accurate is that they are sharing information with me they otherwise would have absolutely no knowledge of. And even though the readings are coming from different parts of the country, from people who do not know each other, the information is always consistent.

But in addition to psychics, clairvoyants, and angel ladies, there is another category of individuals I have met that comprise people who hold a very special place in my heart. I can only describe this category of individuals to you by calling them "ascended masters." They are very close to the top of the mountain, very close to having reached their destination. They are highly gifted, and the words they speak are profound. Their ability to channel information from the spiritual world is also extraordinary. It truly is a blessing to share in their energy field and many of them are gifted healers.

Many of you have requested information in the past as to how to have your own angelic reading by phone. If you do have that desire, you may contact us at the address shown on the last page of this book, and we will provide you with the name and phone numbers of individuals who you can call for your own personal reading. We also publish this information in our monthly newsletter, *The Messenger: News of the Great Tomorrow*.

Chapter
- 6 -
God

I have a vision of God being on top of a mountain. And each and every one of you are traversing that mountain, traveling up the road to reach the top and be at one with God. The vehicle you are traveling in is your religious beliefs, your metaphysical beliefs, your value systems, how you conduct your way of life. But when you reach a certain height as you get closer to the top of the mountain, you abandon the vehicle in which you are traveling, for you no longer want to be restricted to dogma and doctrine. Having reached that height, you find that your relationship with God is one that is truly spiritual, that we are all truly brothers and sisters, not only with our words and thoughts, but also in our deeds.

What is your image of God? Is your image the same as that of Isaiah in the Old Testament? When you think of God, do you envision a handsome elderly man with long white hair and a beard, sitting on a throne, wearing a soft-colored robe? Is that not your image?

But what if God does not have white hair? What if God has short black hair, such as a crew cut? And what if, instead of being elderly, God's appearance is of a twenty-year-old, clean shaven? And instead of a long robe, God is wearing a sweatshirt and jeans?

Or what if, instead, God does have long hair and wears a robe? And what if God also wears lipstick because instead of being a man, God is a beautiful woman?

You may envision God in any manner you choose, but none would be accurate—or, if you prefer, all would be accurate. For, although you cannot see God, you experience God in everything that you can see.

God can be experienced through the beautiful sunrise of a Phoenix valley morning, or the magnificent sunset of a Hawaiian island, or in the majestic snow-capped mountains of Colorado. God can be experienced in the wondrous national parks in California, the extraordinary waterfalls of upstate New York, the huge lakes in the Northern Midwest, the sandy beaches of the southeastern United States. God can be experienced in the giant forests of the Pacific Northwest, the expansive plains of Texas, and in the beautiful multicolored faces of the people who walk among the high-rises of the crowded downtown streets of New York, Paris, London, and Rome.

In all of these, and in millions and millions of other scenes throughout the world, you can experience God. For God Himself and Herself cannot be seen, but only experienced. It is impossible for us, in our human form, to truly see God. But we can experience God in every moment of our lives, through everything that we can see, feel, hear, and touch that is good, that brings us happiness, joy, serenity, peace, pleasure, and comfort, for it is a manifestation of God.

Some will tell you: reach out and find God, search above you and around you, and find God. I say to you: look within and find God, for God truly does reside within you.

Do you know that the only reason that you are alive at this moment is because the spirit of God is within you?

Otherwise, you would not exist in this material world. You are alive because you are a part of God.

Before you came on to this earth plane, you existed in the spirit dimension. You were, and are, a child of God. God created you from God's spirit. Your relationship to God is that of a tree to a forest, as a drop of water is to a lake, a grain of sand is to a beach. You are a part of the whole. You are part of the Creator. You are part of the Divinity. You are part of God. You are not a human being, that by coincidence, has a spirit and soul. You are spirit with a soul that is having a human experience.

In one of the chapters of *The Messengers*, Julia Ingram asks me while I am under hypnosis and in the memory of Paul, how Jeshua would describe God. I answered her, through the memory of Paul, as follows:

> *Jeshua says that even though we often refer to God as the Father, that God is both the Father and the Mother. And that God has no single gender. That God is a force, an entity of love and life—and all of us are a part of Him. Think of a body of water, like a lake. And that lake, for purpose of understanding, is an energy force of love and wisdom in all of us. Each drop of that lake is part of the whole. And then we take a jar and dip it into a lake, which was made up of thousands and thousands of little drops of water. These are part of the whole of that lake. We then scatter the drops in different places. Each little drop is put into the body of a new born. Inside each of those people would be part of that lake, even if they do not recognize it. And that little part of that lake is eternal, is everlasting, and is part of the total, is part of that lake. And it is what gives us life. And when that little part of that lake leaves the body, the body no longer has life. Now, if we equate that lake, instead to being God, a different form of energy, rather than a lake, we will have a better*

understanding of why Jeshua says that we are part of God, just as that drop of water was once part of the lake. And if that drop of water were to return eventually to the lake, it would then be again at one with the rest of the lake. So it is when our spirit becomes at one again, someday, not only in thought, but physically in God, that we are again at one with God.

You are multi-dimensional, in that part of you, that part that you are "consciously" aware of, functions in the dimension of the material world. But the other part of you, that which is your spirit and soul, functions within the other dimension simultaneously with the material world, in what we call the spiritual world.

What does it mean that you are multi-dimensional? Your physical body is corporeal, for it can be touched and seen. But who you truly are as a person is represented by your personality, your intellect, your emotions, and your values. That is really who you are as a person.

What is the relationship between your spirit and soul? Your spirit is everlasting. Your spirit is immortal. Your spirit is a part of God. It can never change, for it is God. But your soul is the personality, the intellect, the memories, and the values of your spirit. Your soul can change with every human experience that you have in your life. That is the relationship between your spirit and your soul.

But God is not multi-dimensional. God is exclusively, unequivocally not a duality, but a manifestation of love. Can one who knows only love be capable of punishing? Can one who generates only love cause heartache or hardship? God can only manifest love, for God is love.

When you come to understand that there is no such thing as death, you come to understand God. When you come to understand there is no such thing as the monster Fear, you come to understand God. When you come to understand that God is our Father and Mother and that every one of us is a child of God, you come to understand God. When you come to understand that, if every one of us is a child of God, then we are all brothers and sisters, then you come to understand God.

There are three ways to acknowledge God. They are through your intellect; through attending services in a house of God, a church; and through living your life in accordance with the will of God.

The first way, through the intellect, is a process in which you come to the conclusion that there must be a God. But even though you may acknowledge intellectually there is a God, this does not mean you truly understand, comprehend, and have a relationship with God.

Attending church also does not necessarily create for you the intimate relationship with God that allows you to recognize that God does reside within you. Even if you have learned to stand up at the right times, sit down at the right times, and memorize all the right places to say amen, and spend the one-and-a-half hours weekly in a church, these actions alone do not provide you an intimate relationship with God. It is only through living your life in accordance with God's will, which I shall discuss in a later chapter, that you are able to truly have that relationship with God that you seek. Obviously, it is possible to recognize and acknowledge God from all three of these methods, but not through the first two without the third.

I once asked the angels, how is it that I have been chosen for this mission, since I do not even have a formal religion? And they answered me, "What religion do you think God is? Do you think God is Presbyterian, Quaker, or Mennonite? God also does not have a formal religion, but embraces all religions that teach God's messages."

And when you provide love and compassion to your brothers and sisters, you yourself, are manifesting God. When you come to understand that our bodies are nurtured by food and rest, but our spirits and souls are nurtured by experiencing love and compassion, then you come to understand and know God.

Chapter
- 7 -
Death

Six years ago I developed a casual friendship with a priest. My relationship was not religious, since I do not have a formal religion. I met him through a friend, and I truly enjoyed being in his company. The few times we saw each other, we never discussed religion. He had no knowledge of my background, my experiences, or my belief system, for the relationship predated both my angelic experiences and the writing of *The Messengers*. So, I had never discussed with him those areas that I had assumed would never become, as they have today, public knowledge. One day I learned he was going to be required to have a bypass heart operation. I called him on the phone and invited him to lunch three days before his operation, to provide him encouragement and moral support. When I began to discuss his forthcoming operation, I saw discomfort in his body and fear in his eyes.

I asked him why he was afraid and he responded, "What if I die?" And I said, "But surely, in your position, you do not fear death, do you?"

He hesitated before answering, and he painfully responded by asking, "What if God does not love me? What if I do not go to heaven?" I looked into his eyes, searching for truth. "Are you afraid that you will possibly no longer exist after death?" And he quietly and embarrassingly answered, "Yes."

I did not feel, at that time, that I should try to provide him comfort through my own personal experiences. I was concerned that it may require too great of a leap for him. So I decided to share with him my knowledge of near-death experiences (NDEs), knowledge that I had acquired in talking to individuals who had NDEs, and also from the books that I had read. I explained to him how people from all walks of life, of different religions, including those who had no religious beliefs, all had the same experiences when they had their NDE.

I told him about the hundreds of cases I had read of individuals leaving their bodies at the time of death and being able to describe the events that took place in the operating room of the hospital, the activities of the nurses and the doctors, the words that they spoke—scenes described by the person even though they had temporarily died and could not have otherwise witnessed the events. I shared with him that all of those who have had this experience, tell of being drawn to a magnificent light, which then propelled them through a tunnel, until they entered the light at the other end of the tunnel. Some were met by light beings, and some by their loved ones who had passed on before them.

My clergical friend listened with great fascination, his eyes shining with hope. He had no previous knowledge of what I was sharing with him, and I could sense his gratitude and the release of some of his fear. The next day I delivered to him a book I had read that contained many different cases of NDEs, that had been carefully and professionally documented through the research of the author.

I visited my friend at the hospital the day after his operation. I found him lying in bed with a big smile on his face and my book lying on the table by his bedside. He took my hand in his and genuinely thanked me for the book, my concerns, and the words of comfort I had shared with him. What had made a major impression on me at that time was that here was a man of the cloth, a man who had spent years of his life in religious training and preparation, a man who preached the words of God on a weekly basis to his congregation, and yet he feared death, the possibility of the extinction of his mind, his memories, his spirit.

When I was very young, I developed an insight. I realized that everybody wanted to go to heaven, but nobody wanted to die first. But as I grew older, and my understanding was further developed, I discovered the reason why that was so. What is the thing that people fear more than anything else in life? I discovered that it was death.

People are frightened that it is possible that death may represent oblivion. What if, in reality, there is no afterworld, there is no spiritual world, but instead, we are born into this world by accident—that we are just members of another species, and like an ant, a frog, a mouse, a horse, or an elephant, when we die, we no longer continue to exist in any form whatsoever, for we then become extinct?

To no longer exist, would that not be the same as never having existed? To have no memories of your loved ones, to have no memories of your past accomplishments and failures, victories and defeats, deeds and misdeeds... would that not be the same as if they had never taken place?

But I share with you that I know with all my heart and soul, there is no such thing as death. There is only transition. Your spirit and soul are like an indestructible jewel, and your body is a jewel box within which the jewel is contained. Even though in time the box will deteriorate and wear out, the jewel is perpetual and everlasting.

For those of you who are doubters and do fear death, I wish it was possible for me to transfer the experiences I have had to you. I wish there was a magic button that I could press that would enable you to have the comfort and serenity that is in my mind and my heart, because of what I have been exposed to, so that you will also have the absolute proof, beyond any means and doubts, that God does exist, that the spiritual world does exist, that we are perpetual and everlasting, and that there is no such thing as death. There are only transitions.

I truly believe that those who do not believe in a spiritual world or afterlife, such as scientists who claim that evolution does not allow room for God and the spiritual world, or atheists who deny the existence of God and immortality, are in reality crying out for proof of just the opposite. They desperately are hoping others will show them evidence that they are wrong. And the more adamant they are at professing their beliefs, whether they be academic, or based on science, emotion, or theories, beneath the surface of their proclamations there is a desperate silent cry to be proven wrong.

I know with all my heart and soul that there will be events that will happen worldwide as we proceed into the next millennium that will give greater affirmation to those who are believers, that will erase the skepticism of those who are skeptics, and that will greatly affect the beliefs of the nonbelievers—events that can only be interpreted as miracles and that will prove that God is intervening in our lives. There will be no other explanations.

The greatest hardship for us while we are alive in the physical world is the loss of our loved ones. We experience so much pain and anguish when we lose loved ones. We not only mourn the absence of their company, but we also ask for the comfort of knowing if they are still with us in the spiritual world.

I have come to understand the process, partially through my own experiences, through answers provided to me while in age-regression hypnotherapy; partially through answers given to me by "spirit," the knowledge and wisdom from that realm of God, Jeshua, and the angels; and partially from the answers given to me from what I refer to as "my higher self." But the answers and information have always been consistent, and I know them to be true. I hope you are also able to have the comfort of embracing these truths.

When our loved ones' spirits and souls leave their bodies, the spirits do go towards the light and pass through the tunnel, to be greeted by God's guides as well as their own loved ones who have passed before them. While in the spiritual world, they are totally aware of our activities, our anguish, and the love that we have for them. They themselves do not feel pain or anguish, for they realize those emotions we are experiencing as a part of mortal life are temporal and transitory. They understand those emotions are emanating from our love and not from our indifference, hostility, or lack of caring. Every human emotion we experience has an impact on our soul, and they know that the sorrow we experience over missing our loved ones' company is not a negative emotion, but instead is emanating from love.

But for the loved ones who are now in spirit, they are in God's light. They are experiencing joy, happiness, serenity . . . and are basking in the universal consciousness of God's love. While they appreciate the feelings that we have for them, emanating from what we consider "our loss," they do not want us to feel despair, do not want us to hurt, do not want us to feel grief. If they were able to talk directly to you, they would say, "Please understand that I am not experiencing pain, not experiencing sadness, not experiencing anxieties. I am in ecstasy. I am in bliss. I am joyful and grateful for your love, but also for the knowledge that I am now at home with God. Know that I love you, and I know of the love you have for me. I shall be with you often."

At times you will feel your loved ones' presence. They may come to you in your dreams, and during your meditations. They know that they are in your thoughts and your prayers. But the most important thing you should know is that your loved ones want you to enjoy life. The greatest gift you can give to them is to continue on, loving them, missing them, but allowing their love to be an inspiration to you. And, through that love, to enjoy life every moment and let others enjoy life through you.

If, instead, your love for them is reflected in despair, gloom, and sadness, and you no longer find joy in the gift of experiencing life in the physical world, you are not honoring their love as they would want you to. No one who loves another wants that love to cause discomfort and heartache to the person they love. And so it is, with your loved ones who have left the physical world and who now reside in spirit. Honor their memories. Treasure your memories. Know that they are still with you, and live life to the fullest, because that is their wish, and that is the most precious way that you can show your love for them.

The beginning of birth opens an incredible door into a room called life. The room is a maze, filled with many obstacles and challenges. When we reach the other side of the room, we find another door that takes us into the spiritual world. Occasionally, by accident, or by circumstances outside of our control, we fall through a crack in the floor, as we make our way through the maze, and we enter into the spiritual world before we have completed our way through the room and have found the door.

There are times in our lives when we will find our loved ones in pain or suffering caused from disease, sickness, or accident. Even though we pray for their survival, oftentimes they will have their spirit and soul leave their body and go into spirit. It is important that you understand, no matter how difficult it may be to understand, that death is the ultimate healing. When the body is in so much pain and discomfort and is experiencing the greatest hardship in functioning, regardless of the cause of that hardship, the ultimate healing is the spirit leaving the body.

Friends of mine recently gave birth to a child who has Down's syndrome. This beautiful child is having great difficulty continuing. She has troubles with her lungs. My wife recently asked me, "Nick, will she make it?" And I answered her that, "It is not her physician's decision, it is not her parent's decision, nor is it God's decision. It is the child's decision. Within her little tiny body is a spirit and soul. It is a spirit with the wisdom of the soul mind that will make the decision. We must honor and respect whatever decision she makes."

As for yourself, as you approach the departure of your spirit from this earthplane, prepare yourself mentally and spiritually. Do away with your anxieties and reinforce in your mind that you are a child of God and that you are returning to your spiritual home. Do not show fear, but rather love, to those around you. Tell them that you love them and cherish them and that you want them to celebrate your memory rather than mourning over you, that you want them to enjoy life to the fullest, rather than feeling gloom and despair.

You know that you will soon be in the kingdom of God. You have nothing to fear. Remember, our minds can make a heaven out of hell, and a hell out of heaven. You must control your mind and focus on God's love. It is so important that you make the transition in love and not in fear. And reinforce that understanding to your loved ones. Share with them that you want them to enjoy their lives to the fullest, and that you will always be with them. The greatest gift you can give to them is to share this wisdom and strength, not only verbally, but in writing or on a video or tape. They will cherish it forever, until they, in time, join you to be with you and God.

Chapter
- 8 -
Jeshua

If Jeshua were here with us today, not only in spirit, which he is, but also in physical body, what would he say to us? Would he be proud of us? Would he commend and applaud the teachers and preachers of his word? Or would he ask, "Why have you strayed, my brothers and sisters? Why have you used my name to prejudice the lives of others, to polarize one another? And why have you tortured, maimed, and killed your brothers and sisters in my name?"

Jeshua would say to you, "The Lord is our Father and Mother, and we are all children of God. And is it not true that, if we are all the children of a common Father and Mother, we are therefore all brothers and sisters?"

Jeshua would share with you that he is a spiritual guide for any who choose to have him as a spiritual guide. It does not make a difference whether you are Buddhist, Hindu, Jewish, Christian, practice no religion, and, yes, even whether you are agnostic. He is willing to be the spiritual guide of any who ask him to help them to reach our destination in our journey, to be at one with God. Jeshua never intended that he be confined to be the spiritual guide for only one religion.

We are all on the same journey, even though we arrive at our destination at different times. The journey that we are on is as if we are traveling on an ocean, all of us trying to reach the same destination. And the vessel that we are in, comprises our religious beliefs, our spiritual beliefs, our value systems, and our way of life. To some, the journey is a glorious one. The sky is pastel blue, the weather is balmy, the ocean is calm, and we bathe in God's light as we get closer and closer to our destination. To others, the weather is stormy, the ocean is hostile and ferocious, the journey is filled with chaos, confusion, and discomfort. At times we may lose the direction in which we are traveling and actually find ourselves having strayed off course, getting further away rather than closer to our destination. And if we have Jeshua as our spiritual guide, he can put us back on course, to enjoy the journey as God intended.

But our Beloved Brother's ego does not threaten you or demand of you that you accept him to be your spiritual guide or that otherwise you would not find God. And even though some will find greater enjoyment while on the journey than others, we shall all eventually find our way to God. Did not Paul say in his letter to the Romans that all who call upon the name of the Lord will be saved? And by saved, he meant we would be acknowledged by God and accepted by God.

In *The Messengers*, through the memory of Paul, I shared with you details of the life of Jeshua not known before in our modern history. I have been asked many times, how do historians react to the information in *The Messengers* that they have never seen, written, or spoken of before? How do they react to those areas that are in conflict with the Gospels?

I have come to realize that those who are referred to as historians are, in reality, not historians in the same sense as those who are able to document the First World War or the life of Gandhi or Winston Churchill. They have no films to review. They have no magazines to read. They have no eyewitnesses to interview.

The only documents they have as a source regarding Jeshua's life are the Gospels. But what are the Gospels? They are the writings of four individuals, two who were disciples of Jeshua, one who was ten years old when Jeshua died on the cross, and one who was born after Jeshua died on the cross, a Greek who had never lived in Jerusalem.

We must understand that Jeshua died on the cross at the age of thirty-three. For the next thirty-seven years the story of Jeshua was verbally passed down from one person to another, was shared by rote, by constant repetition. In those days, that was the custom, for it was difficult to write, since writings took place on either parchments such as goat skins, or on papyrus, a product made from a plant grown in Egypt.

So the first Gospel to be written, that of Mark, who was a child when Jeshua died, was written in approximately 70 A.D. How accurately could you describe events, if you had to recall them, that took place thirty-seven years earlier? Would you be able to describe conversations, word for word, without the aide of cassette tapes from a recorder or of written notes? Is there any wonder that, through the memory of Paul, I would have provided information in much greater detail, including identifying discrepancies that are found in the Gospels?

Many of those I consider qualifying as historians have told me they are grateful for my information, that it made sense to them, and that it answered many unanswered questions as to what really happened two thousand years ago.

Others have said, " No, you are wrong. Your information cannot be accurate. Your story cannot be true." "And why is that?" I asked. They responded, "Because the information is stated differently in the Gospels. Therefore, you have to be wrong."

I do not intend to argue with those who are in dissent. They say I am wrong, for they are relying on documents that were originally written in ancient Aramaic, at least thirty-seven years after the events took place. The documents were then translated into ancient Greek, then again translated into ancient Latin. Then in the last half of the fourth century, they were translated into contemporary Latin by the pre-medieval church, and it was at this time that they distorted the true messages of Jeshua and Paul, as I shall discuss in a later chapter. Finally, they were transferred into English, fifteen hundred years after the original writing. And that is the basis for their argument? Was not the child warned, "Beware of those who try to open the closet door, to release the monster Fear, for surely they are being influenced by the supernatural evil force, the devil."

I want to share with you the truth of the life of Jeshua. Who was he? How did he live? Why did he die? What were his messages? I share the following with you through the memory of Paul.

It is true that Mary and Joseph lived in Nazareth. Joseph was twenty years older than Mary, thirty-six years old when Jeshua was born. His first wife having died, Joseph was a widower, leaving him with one child, a son named Simon. Simon was a young man at the time of Jeshua's birth. Joseph was a carpenter by trade, fixing broken furniture as well as making simple tables and chairs.

In the Aramaic language they referred to Jeshua as being a "*naggar*." "*Naggar*" can either mean a wise man, a holy man, or a craftsman. In one of the translations, the translator had to make a decision. Was Jeshua a holy man? Obviously he was. Was he a wise man? Obviously he was. Was he a craftsman? Apparently, because Joseph had been a carpenter, the translator made a decision to translate the word *naggar* into the word craftsman. From that time on, the storytellers referred to Jeshua as a carpenter. He was not a carpenter. But he was a wise man, and he was a holy man.

Mary was sixteen years old at the time of the birth of Jeshua. In ancient Aramaic it is written that she was an *almah*, which meant a young woman. *Almah* was then translated to the word *parthenos* in Greek. This word could either mean a young girl or a virgin, or both. When the Gospels were translated from Aramaic, two of the four Gospels referred to her as an *almah*. Over the next hundreds of years, this created a huge fight among the Christian religions. Were they telling us that Jeshua was born to a virgin through divine intervention or to a young girl? It was finally in the nineteenth century, in 1854, that the church decided to end this debate by officially declaring the immaculate conception and the virgin birth as doctrine.

Was there a virgin birth? I do not know. It was not discussed at that time. Paul had never been told by Jeshua of such an event. Do I believe it is possible? Yes, I believe in miracles. I believe that God can and does intervene in our lives.

I must tell you in all honesty, I not only do not know if there was an immaculate conception and a virgin birth, I also do not care. In either case, it does not change what Jeshua was and is, nor does it change the love and respect that I have for Mary. Mary was a petite, very pretty, quiet, gentle, loving person. She did not play an active role in Jeshua's teachings, but she always gave him her loving support.

Jeshua was not raised in Nazareth. He was raised in Capernaum. Capernaum is located on the northwestern shore of the Sea of Galilee. It was from those cities along the western shore of the Sea of Galilee that Jeshua recruited his early followers, the disciples. They came from the lakeshore cities of Capernaum, Magdala, Tiberius, and Bethsaida. That is why they were fishermen, not farmers.

The Sea of Galilee was also known as Lake Tiberius, for it really was a lake, not a sea. During Jeshua's life, the name was changed for a time, to be called Lake Tiberius, after the

Emperor Tiberius. The lake was approximately thirteen miles long and seven miles wide. It was on a hillside, overlooking this lake, in a natural amphitheater that sloped down to the lake where voices could carry for hundreds of feet that Jeshua gave his inspiring "Sermon on the Mount."

As a youngster Jeshua was taught words of wisdom at the Essene colony at Mount Carmel, located in the province of Samaria on the western shore of the Great Sea, which today is called the Mediterranean Sea. Mary had also been taught there as a youngster. It was at this early training ground that Jeshua learned the philosophy of Eastern cultures, which had been indoctrinated into the Essene teachings.

In his early teens, Jeshua also traveled to Egypt and received intensive training in Alexandria. There was a very large Jewish population in Alexandria, which included many respected Jewish scholars. It must be understood that, during that time, in the three provinces of Palestine in which Jeshua lived and traveled, it was only the Judaic religion that existed, along with those who were pagans or worshiped idols, or, as Paul often remarked, prayed to lemon trees.

The three provinces of Palestine were: Galilee, located in the north; Samaria, south of Galilee; and Judea, which included the wonderful holy city of Jerusalem and the town of Bethlehem. Galilee was a land of fertile and rolling hills, lush with vegetation and rivers and valleys. Galilee was rich in agriculture and fishing, being a major source of the food supply for the large population of Jerusalem. It was here in Galilee that Jeshua began his ministry, in the smaller cities and towns along the west bank of the Sea of Galilee, as well as further inland. Galilee was also a quasi-independent kingdom, not a province of the Roman Empire.

The province of Samaria was less populated and was very arid. Jeshua traveled along the roads of this desert-like portion of Palestine. And it was here that he was to be found in the smaller cities of Sychar, Samaria, and Antipatris, places where Jeshua stopped and preached when he made his frequent journeys between his home in Capernaum and the great city of Jerusalem, where he made his greatest impact. The Jewish people of Galilee and Samaria were not as pious as those in the province of Judea, because the two northern provinces had been occupied in previous years by the conquering armies of the Persians and the Babylonians. Many of the soldiers stationed there then remained in these provinces, marrying local women of the Jewish faith. This resulted in a less intense observation of the Jewish religion in those two provinces, as opposed to the practice of the faith in Jerusalem and Bethlehem and in other cities in the province of Judea.

Within the city of Jerusalem, which consisted of over three hundred thousand people, was the most magnificent temple in the world. I will refer to it as the Temple of Solomon, for it was built on the site of the temple that was first built by King Solomon nine hundred years earlier and that later was destroyed. This extraordinary structure was being built by King Herod during the life of Jeshua. Even at the time of Jeshua's death, there was still additional construction taking place, although it was, for practical purposes, a completed temple in 33 A.D.

It was here at the porticos and the steps of this magnificent temple that a young Paul would listen to the debates of his fellow citizens, sometimes sitting in the shade of the temple or in the opposite side in the sunlight, depending on the time of year and the time of the day. It was here in the temple that Paul eventually committed acts that caused him to be arrested, which I shall refer to in the chapter on Paul. And it was here that Jeshua taught his ministry, which eventually would be heard by millions and millions of people over the next two thousand years.

What was Jeshua like? Was he human or a deity? Was he truly the son of God?

When Jeshua was hungry, he ate. When he was thirsty, he drank. When he was tired, he rested. Jeshua had the same physical needs that you and I do, and he had an incredible sense of humor. He loved to be around people, people from all walks of life. His social relationships were never distinguished by wealth or power. He loved all people equally, for it was the minds and hearts of people that attracted Jeshua to them, not their gold or material possessions.

But there was another side of Jeshua beyond his human nature. Was he the son of God? Without any question. But I also know that Jeshua believed, as I also know to be true, that we are all children of God. All of us are the sons and daughters of God.

What distinguished Jeshua from every other person was that he had already reached perfection. He did not have to come back to live on earth again. He was a gift from God. That is why he had the incredible wisdom that he did. That is why he was able to do miracles, for he came onto earth as an already perfected soul. His spiritual mind and his conscious mind were one and the same.

Even in the Gospel of John, it is said that Jeshua was teaching in a small temple in Nazareth and made reference to Abraham, who had lived many hundreds of years earlier. It stated that Abraham had rejoiced at something that Jeshua previously did. And the people challenged him. They said, "What are you talking about? Abraham lived many hundreds of years ago, and you are a young man." And Jeshua answered them, "I say to you in truth, before Abraham was, I lived."

The preachers of religion who do not know the truth, that reincarnation was the "absolute" belief of the Jews at the time of Jeshua, will vehemently argue that Jeshua meant something else other than that he had lived before Abraham. They desperately try to explain differently the words found in the Gospel of John, for example, by saying he meant he lived in spirit, or that he meant that he was God, or some other explanation. But his words are what they are. Jeshua said he lived before Abraham, and Abraham, who was the father of the Judaic religion, had rejoiced at Jeshua's actions at that time. Yes, God has blessed us with his gift, the life of our beloved brother, who came to us as a perfected soul.

What was the purpose of Jeshua being born again if he had already reached perfection? Pretend that you are lost in the jungle, and you are surrounded by poisonous snakes. There are ferocious animals wanting to kill you, and there is quicksand. You are told you must get out of this danger in twenty minutes, or you would surely lose your life. And you have absolutely no idea how to get out of this dangerous situation.

Pretend that all of a sudden Jeshua appeared before you, and said, "Follow me. I shall show you the way." And you followed his path, and twenty minutes later you were in complete safety. Is it not true that by following him, he saved your life? Is it not true that by following his path, he showed you the way? That is what Jeshua still offers to us today. It is your choice, if you wish to have him as your spiritual guide on your journey to be at one with God.

The Gospels tell us of the life of Jeshua beginning as an adult, in his early thirties, when he began to do his miracles. The historians speak of the years before that as his lost years. They do not know what he was doing before he began to do his miracles.

As I shared with you in detail in *The Messengers*, Paul met Jeshua at the age of twenty-one, when Jeshua was twenty-three. Jeshua spent those earlier years of his ministry traveling the three provinces of Palestine, teaching his messages. But it was not until he began to do his miracles of healing in his early thirties that he began to have a major impact on the people of Jerusalem. It was only then that people by the thousands flocked to hear Jeshua speak on the steps of the magnificent holy temple in Jerusalem. And it was only then that they realized that Jeshua was not just another preacher, but was a special son of God.

There were three major events that made such an impact on the people of Judea that enables us to know of our beloved brother's teachings today. The first was his decision to do healings. Surely, is not one whose words are so powerful, whose wisdom is so great, whose presence is so sacred that he can heal the spirit and souls of his brothers and sisters—must he not be the anointed one? It was through his healings that people began to open their hearts and souls to the special messages Jeshua shared with them. It was through his healings that he was able to separate himself from the many hundreds of teachers who preached the words of God two thousand years ago.

The second major event in Jeshua's life that changed his course and that of history was "the raising of Lazarus from the dead." Lazarus lived with his two sisters, Martha and Mary, in the town of Bethany. Their home was located about a twenty-five-minute walk south of the city of Jerusalem. Whenever Jeshua came into Jerusalem, almost without exception, he stayed in the home of Lazarus and Mary. Mary was known as Mary Magdalene, because the family originally came from the city of Magdala, on the western shore of the Sea of Galilee, just south of Capernaum. Magdala, at that time, was an active fishing community with over thirty thousand people. Today it is a sleepy Arab town of approximately five thousand people.

There is a story in the Gospels of Jeshua saving the life of a prostitute named Mary, who was being stoned by the people for her acts of indiscretion. Some of the historians have confused this prostitute Mary, with Mary of Magdala (Mary Magdalene). They were not the same person.

Mary was a loving, gentle, beautiful woman. She had long black hair, an olive complexion, large brown eyes and an athletic body. Jeshua and Mary loved each other. I truly believe they would have married one day, if Jeshua had not given his life on the cross when he did.

Why was she called Mary Magdalene? In those days people did not have last names. In the community where they were born and raised with their family, they were called by their given name and the name of their father, to separate them from others. If you knew four Simons, one may be called Simon the son of Aaron, another would be Simon the son of Jacob, and so on. That was how they were able to distinguish themselves, providing their father was also known in that city. But if they lived in a city where people did not know their father, they instead, would be referred to by their name and the city of their place of origin. People in Jerusalem did not know Joseph, who had died when Jeshua was a teenager. Therefore, they called him Jeshua from Nazareth, since that was where his parents lived when he was born. That is also why they called Paul, Paul of Tarsus, and why they called Mary, Mary Magdalene, just as you might call a person from Boston, a Bostonian.

It is said in the Gospels that Lazarus died, and three days later Jeshua raised him from the dead. In *The Messengers*, I shared with you that Paul did not know, if indeed, Lazarus had died and Jeshua had brought him back to life, or if Lazarus had been in a state of unconsciousness, what we would call a coma, and Jeshua had revived him. It makes no difference to me which of the two actually happened. In either case, it does not change who Jeshua was and who Jeshua is. However, to the people of Jerusalem, as the word spread that Jeshua had brought Lazarus back from the dead, thousands and thousands of people flocked to see, touch, and hear this special "holy man," he who had the incredible power "to raise the dead." It was then that the Romans became concerned that there was a man in Jerusalem who was a threat to their mission and a threat to Pontius Pilate, the leading Roman authority living in Jerusalem.

Was it not the responsibility of the Romans to control the people of Jerusalem, so they could collect and send their annual taxes back to the treasury of Rome? That was the only reason Roman soldiers occupied Jerusalem as well as the other territories and countries they had conquered or that had submitted to the power of Rome.

The Romans controlled the people of Jerusalem by two means. The first was through the seventy-man council of religious leaders known as the Sanhedrin. They looked to the Sanhedrin to control the religious zealots and preachers of that area. In Jeshua's case, the Romans recognized that Jeshua functioned outside the influence of the Sanhedrin, totally independent of any religious authority, although he was a Jew.

The second method of control by the Romans was through their brutality. The Romans ruled in the most heartless and ruthless way. They killed hundreds and hundreds of Jews every year who they felt were a threat to their mission. If they decided to kill a person without making an example of him, they brought the person to a swift death by beheading. If they wished to make an example of that person or to severely punish the person, they did it by the brutal act of crucifixion, where the person's followers could visually watch, in anguish and pain, the crucified one die in slow agony on the cross.

In Jeshua's case, following the tremendous response he received by the thousands after the revival of Lazarus, the Romans made a decision to act swiftly in arresting Him.

The Gospels say that Jeshua was arrested on the evening following the Last Supper. The Gospels differ as to what night the Last Supper actually took place. Obviously, the memories of the two disciples who were Gospel writers, Matthew and John, were different. Mark's memory as to which night it took place is not relevant, since he was not a disciple, which comes from the ancient word discipulus, meaning a pupil. He was only ten years old at that time.

Luke's history of that night should also be discounted, for, unlike the other Gospel writers, he was not of the Jewish faith. The other three were Jewish Christians, but Luke was a gentile Christian, born after Jeshua had died on the cross. He was a Greek who never lived in Jerusalem and did not speak Hebrew or Aramaic. He would not have had personal knowledge of the Last Supper.

Information that Luke wrote in the New Testament, both in his Gospels and in the section referred to as Acts, is information that he received from others and his own interpretations and slants on events that took place. Luke visited with Paul often during the last several years of Paul's life, and Paul continually had a problem with Luke. Paul respected and dearly loved his colleagues, those who accepted the teachings and became Christians, regardless of whether they were Jewish Christians who accepted Jeshua, or pagans who had accepted Jeshua, and in so doing, like Luke, had become Gentile Christians. But Luke could not identify with the Jewish Christians. He was rude to them. And because they revered God through their religious foundation of Judaism, Luke was actually anti-Semitic. This troubled Paul greatly. It often tainted the words of Luke. This is why there are errors in the scriptures known as Acts, because Luke created his own version of what actually happened two thousand years ago, rather than providing the true facts. I shall discuss this in a later chapter called "Paul."

So the Gospels of John and Matthew differ as to when the Last Supper took place. As described in detail in *The Messengers*, I shall share with you the true story.

Zebedee was the father of the disciples John and James. Zebedee was a man of substantial wealth who owned a fleet of fishing boats in the Sea of Galilee. Prior to becoming disciples, his two sons managed his business for him as fishermen. Zebedee had a home in the city of Jerusalem in addition to the one on the western coast of the Sea of

Galilee. The Last Supper took place in the upper floor of his home in Jerusalem. Matthew was right. It occurred the first night of the Jewish holiday called Passover. The ceremony that took place at the Last Supper was similar to that which took place in homes of Jews all over the world two thousand years ago and that still takes place today in homes of those who are still adhering strictly to the Jewish faith.

What is the holiday and dinner ceremony of Passover? Twelve hundred years earlier, the Jews were in bondage by the Egyptians. They had been conquered in war and were the slaves of the Egyptians. Through the leadership of Moses, the Jews demanded their freedom, but the Egyptians refused.

The Bible tells the story of Moses, who, through the power of God, brought one plague after another upon the Egyptians who refused to liberate the Jewish slaves. Finally, we were told that Moses instructed every Jewish family to place the blood of a lamb above their door and that the Angel of Death would "pass over" their homes. But from the homes of the Egyptians the Angel of Death would take the lives of their first-born sons. It was only after that, that the Egyptians allowed freedom to the Jews, who then crossed the Red Sea to wander through the desert under the leadership of Moses until they returned to the Holy Land of Jerusalem. And in commemoration of that event, freeing the Jewish people from slavery, Jews celebrate the holiday of Passover every year beginning with a ceremonial supper.

It is during that ceremony that certain rituals are performed, such as the eating of unleavened bread and spices and drinking of ceremonial wine. Again, the Gospels of Matthew and John, who were the only two Gospel writers who were at the Last Supper, differ. Matthew described the ceremony of Jeshua dipping the bread and offering it to be consumed by the others as the eating of his flesh and the drinking of the wine to symbolize the drinking of his blood. This was the creation of the practice of the Eucharist, which is still performed by millions and millions of Christians throughout the world today. John does not discuss this ceremony.

I do not know what version of the Gospel is accurate, for Paul was not there at the Last Supper. Paul was not a disciple. If you are one who does honor the practice of the Eucharist, I say God bless you. It is in honor of Jeshua, and in either case, it does not change who Jeshua was and is.

That evening following the supper, the Romans arrested Jeshua. The next day the Romans crucified him. Only the Romans had the power of capital punishment. Only the Romans had the power to take another's life. The Jewish authorities could only practice civil law, such as trying people for theft or destruction of another's property. Only the Romans had the ability and power to take the life of our beloved brother.

At the time the Gospels were being written, beginning with Mark's, sixteen thousand Roman troops were killing thousands of Jews who wanted their freedom from Roman occupation. It was at that time in history that the Romans destroyed and tore down the most beautiful temple in the world, the Holy Temple in Jerusalem. And then Jerusalem became a Roman city for the next several hundred years.

When the Gospels were written, the writers feared that if they specifically named and held the Romans accountable and responsible for the killing of Jeshua, the apostles would also most likely be killed, which many of them were anyway, and the teaching of Christianity would come to an immediate halt. So, they tried to soften the situation by implying that the decision to take the life of Jeshua was made by the Jewish leaders of the Council of Sanhedrin and that the Romans reluctantly complied with the Jewish leaders. The Roman scholars embellished on this in the fourth century when they embraced Christianity. The premedieval church did not want the Roman Empire to take responsibility for the crucifixion of Jeshua.

The deception described above was unfortunate, for the three Gospel writers who were Jewish Christians did not realize that, in their attempt to protect themselves, they planted the seed of anti-Semitism. They did not anticipate that millions and millions of Jews over the next two thousand years would be discriminated against and, in some cases, tortured and put to death. This would happen at different times in history, because of the accounting of the events that took place regarding the crucifixion of Jeshua. It is time to put an end to the polarization of people, to the prejudice and discrimination against brothers and sisters being performed in the name of Jeshua. I pray to God that the religious leaders throughout the world will have the courage to correct the situation and, in the name and the memory of our beloved brother Jeshua, will influence people to stop discriminating against and killing others because of religious differences.

I have often been asked, what did Jeshua look like? Was his skin dark or light? Did he have blue eyes or brown eyes? Did he look like the paintings we see of him?

In 1996, I had an opportunity to visit one of the finest art museums in the world, in the city of London. There were dozens and dozens of paintings of Jeshua in the Renaissance section of the museum. Every one of them was different. The only thing they had in common was that he had long hair and a beard, as did all adults during his time.

What did Jeshua look like? At that time, there were twelve different tribes of Judaic heritage. Each had their own characteristics, just as in Europe the Italians, French, Irish, and Spanish all have their own characteristics. Jeshua was a descendent from the tribe of David, in which the people were fair-skinned and blue-eyed.

Jeshua had thick brown hair that he parted in the middle. His hair had golden highlights from the sun. He had high cheek bones and a thin face, with wide eyes that were bluish gray in color. He had a thin nose and full lips; his hair and his beard were always well groomed, and his light skin was tanned from his constantly being in the sun. Jeshua had beautiful features. He was a handsome man, but at the same time you could see the tremendous strength in his looks and you could recognize his charisma.

In 1997, I commissioned a very gifted artist to work with me in creating a portrait of Jeshua as he truly looked through the memory of Paul. It took us six months to complete it, but I am thrilled with how we have been able to capture our beloved brother on canvas. We have now made twenty-by-sixteen-inch reproductions of the portrait and offer them through our nonprofit corporation to those who wish to have a portrait of Jeshua.

I wrote earlier that there were three events that changed the course of history, so that we are now able to celebrate the life of Jeshua. The first was Jeshua's decision to do healings; the second was the revival of Lazarus from either death or a coma; the third was the resurrection of Jeshua. People claimed they saw Jeshua walking and talking in the flesh after he died on the cross.

Although Paul did not see Jeshua in the flesh after the crucifixion, I do believe that the resurrection of Jeshua is true. Although Jeshua died on the cross, I believe Jeshua had conquered death, and that, unlike others who had died, his spirit and soul did not leave his body. I believe his spirit remained in his body, and, although he was considered dead and was wrapped in linen cloth and placed in a tomb, his spirit did revive his body, allowing his body to once again live, his heart to beat, his organs to function. I have shared with you earlier that he was a special son of God, that he had come onto earth having already experienced perfection, that his spiritual mind and his conscious mind were one and the same. His soul was pure and Jeshua had conquered death.

As far as ascension, two thousand years ago people believed that heaven existed vertically, above them. They thought the sky had a giant plate above them, which was beyond what the eye could see, and that on the other side of the plate was heaven. That is why they always spoke of ascension as a raising into the heavens, vertically above them. That is why in all the passages of the Bible, heaven is always referred to as being in the sky. That is why they refer to people ascending upwards to heaven and the angels descending from the sky onto the earth below the heavens. Two thousand years ago, they could not envision a spirit world existing in a different dimension. They only understood one dimension, therefore creating a heaven in the sky.

Three hundred and fifty years later the pre-medieval church created hell, based on the dump called Gehenna outside Jerusalem, where people burned their garbage. They had created hell as if it existed under the ground, below the floor of the earth.

But I truly believe that many people throughout the world today understand the concept of the spirit world, and that it is a different dimension than our material world, rather than a geographical location. It is a dimension that functions in a different vibration than the material world dimension, in a different ethereal density.

Did Jeshua die for us? No, he lived for us. Jeshua would never ask us to carry the burden or responsibility for his crucifixion two thousand years ago. He made the decision to make this supreme sacrifice of his life because of his love for God and because of his commitment to his beliefs. Also to the messages he wanted us to accept and embrace today.

Early in 1997, I was doing a radio talk show on a religious station. After being on the air for two hours with the hostess, she informed me that she was going to have a theological doctor join us for the next half hour. He began his remarks to me by stating that he had been listening for the previous two hours and that my information was inaccurate. He stated that 95 percent of the historians agree that the Gospels and the Scriptures are 100 percent accurate.

I knew that his remark was totally false and I asked him, "How can you say that, when even the four Gospel writers disagreed in what took place in the most poignant and saddest moment in history as Jeshua was dying on the cross?"

In the Gospel of Luke, Jeshua speaks from the cross by saying, "Father forgive them; they know not what they do." And he promises the thief who is being crucified alongside of him, "This day thou shalt be with me in Paradise." And then he dies with the words "Father, into thy hands I commend my spirit." And in the Gospel of Matthew, Jeshua states from the cross, "Eli, Eli, lama sabachtani? (My God, my God, why has thou forsaken me?)" And lastly, in the

Gospel of John, his last words were spoken to his mother, "Behold thy mother. I thirst." And he dies with the words "Consummatum est. (It is accomplished.)"

I asked the theological historian, "Is it not true that even in the Gospels the writers differed as to what took place during those painful moments?" He responded by saying, "No, no. It would be the same if two people were watching a circus parade go by. And after it was over, if you asked them what they saw, one person may say that he saw the clowns and the other that he saw the monkeys. It is possible that different people saw different things." I responded by saying that I could not equate the most poignant moment in history, the death of Jeshua on the cross, with the watching of a parade.

I say it is wrong for any religious preacher or teacher to try to place a burden of guilt on anybody by preaching that any person is responsible for the crucifixion of Jeshua two thousand years ago. Why would any religious teacher do this? Would Jeshua want to torment and burden the soul of his brother and sister with this assertion? Would God want to trouble the mind, heart, and soul of his children by preaching to them that they are responsible today for the cruel, brutal death of our brother two thousand years ago?

The greatest lie one could commit is to commit a lie in the name of God. The greatest crime a person can commit is to commit a crime in the name of God. The greatest sin a person can commit is to commit a sin in the name of God.

Jeshua lived for us, not died for us. Jeshua wants you to experience his love and compassion, not his pain and agony. Jeshua offered himself to you to follow his path, to guide you through the difficulties of life, and to help you have a loving understanding with that part inside of you that is God. Not to cause you pain, burden, guilt, and heartache.

Jeshua loves you. He is your brother.

Chapter
- 9 -
Paul

In 1997 a newspaper featured an article about me for their Christmas edition. My face was on its front cover. The article quoted a theologian who stated that I could not have chosen a better historical religious figure to accomplish my objective than Paul. The implication was that I had gone through a selection process and then chose, as the person I would identify as having been the reincarnation of, the apostle Paul.

The truth is that what took place was the total opposite. I had absolutely no knowledge of who Paul was when I began my hypnotic regressions. My only exposure to Paul was hearing his words quoted sometimes in wedding ceremonies. I had never read the Gospels or the Scriptures until after *The Messengers* had been published. I did not select Paul. His spirit and soul selected me.

Do I identify with Paul? I recognize the similarities between us. I recognize that he is a part of me and that we have the same spirit and soul. But I also recognize that although I am today a product of my own environment, I am also on the same mission Paul was on two thousand years ago.

I have now relived a large portion of Paul's life through our collective soul memories. There are occasional occurrences when certain individuals want to argue with me some point about Paul's life. For example, they disagree with me, and they claim that Paul did persecute his fellow Jews. They claim that I am wrong in that he did make a conversion to Christianity on his way to Damascus. They say that he was executed by the Romans rather than, as I know to be the truth, that he died a natural death.

But I have no interest in arguing with these people. I have come to realize that the theologians have no knowledge of who Paul really was other than their own imaginations, other then their own interpretations of his letters. In some cases these letters have been changed by the pre-medieval church and in other cases they have been erroneously translated; in some cases they were letters that he actually did not write and in some cases they are accurate. As for the Scripture's version of Paul's activities, written by Luke in Acts, Luke had his own agenda. He was not there to see the actual events, and he did taint the facts to suit his own bias.

In fact, Luke wrote the following in his Gospel, claiming these words to have been spoken by Jeshua: "Who ever does not hate his father and mother, wife and children, brothers and sisters, even life itself, cannot be my disciple." Jeshua never made those remarks. That was not how Jeshua felt. That was how Luke felt about his own life. But these false remarks of Luke created many problems in the early Christian movement for almost three hundred years, causing many Romans to believe Christianity to be a threat to their families.

Since *The Messengers* has been printed, I have read a number of different versions of who Paul actually was. One theologian concluded he was a small man, bald, with a big nose and a limp, and another shared that Paul was a hunchback. Both claims emanated from Paul's remarks about the "weakness of his flesh" and "the thorn in his side." Another was positive he was gay, because of Paul "erroneously" being accused of discriminating against women. They were all wrong, so wrong.

I will share with you the life of Paul, his motivations, his goals, his dreams, his faults, and his habits. I will share with you both the strengths and the truths that have been distorted, as well as those distortions. Come with me on my journey, back two thousand years ago.

Paul was born in the region of Celicia, in the city of Tarsus. At that time, Tarsus had the same status as Athens and Antioch. Tarsus was located on a plain surrounded by the Tarsus Mountains on its north and the Mountains of Amanus on its east. The River Cyndus flowed from the Tarsus Mountains through a gorge, through the city, and eventually into the Great Sea, which today is called the Mediterranean Sea. Tarsus was located seven miles from the sea. Its land was fertile and it was a port city of substantial wealth. It was a great learning center, including philosophers, poets, and many scholars.

Even though Tarsus was occupied by the Romans, it had a substantial Greek influence, for Alexander the Great had conquered all of the Mediterranean countries, including the area of Tarsus, in 332 B.C. Hellenistic Greek influence had been embedded in Tarsus for several hundreds of years prior to the Roman occupation. Paul was born in 3 A.D., two and a half years after the birth of Jeshua. His father was a man of considerable wealth, owning a large estate with substantial land on the outskirts of the city. In the first seventeen years of Paul's life in Tarsus, he grew up under Roman rule, and that is why he did not look upon the Romans with hostility when he arrived in the Holy Land.

There were three ways for a Jewish family to have Roman citizenship. When the Jews who had been taken into Roman slavery were freed by Pompey in 63 B.C., they were granted citizenship. Citizenship could also be awarded through great acts of merit and achievement benefiting the Roman Empire. And, lastly, it could be purchased at a substantial price. In the case of Paul's family, Roman citizenship had been purchased by his father before Paul was born. That is how Paul became a Roman citizen.

There were many benefits of being a Roman citizen, one that eventually saved Paul's life. As a citizen of Rome, if you were accused of a crime, you had the right to demand trial by a Roman court even if the crime you were accused of, and those making the accusations, were located outside of Rome.

Paul received an excellent education through personal tutors and scholars. At the age of almost eighteen, his education finished, having command of three languages, and being of a strong mind and body, he received permission from his elderly parents to move to the Holy Land. He traveled across the Great Sea, initially to the exciting seaport city of Caesaria, where he stayed for several months, before moving on to the holy city of Jerusalem.

What were Paul's impressions when he arrived in this magical city of Jerusalem, this city of rolling hills, large wealthy homes overlooking the city, and crowded, dirty, noisy winding streets leading into the central marketplaces? Jerusalem was a city built on a hill, a city of marble, stone, domes, spires, narrow cobbled streets, and alleys. It was a city with Roman aquaducts, marketplaces, gardens, villas, red earth, gravel paths, and gray stone walls.

In the poorer section of the city, families would gather in the evening on the flat rooftops of their houses, looking for relief from the heat and conversation with their neighbors. The houses in the crowded downtown area were so close together, one could walk from one flat roof top to another for blocks and blocks. Tiny glassless windows faced the streets, too narrow for a robber to crawl through, yet wide enough for the smoke from the wood-burning braziers that provided heat in the winter to escape to the outside. Huge lanterns, attached to building structures by brackets, were located on the street corners of busy intersections. Their torches were soaked in oil and were lit each evening after sundown. The expensive villas that sat on the hillsides overlooking the city were made of white marble adorned with columns, statues, fountains, atriums, and gardens. These properties were enclosed in white stone walls with gates of iron. The houses were surrounded by sycamore, carob, pine, and palm trees.

Many of the roads were cobblestone, to allow for the movement of horses and carts regardless of weather conditions. The iron tapped soles of the boots of the Roman soldiers could be heard clicking in unison as they marched or trotted through the narrow streets. The sights of Roman soldiers did not disturb Paul. Had he not grown up as a child looking upon the soldiers as his protectors?

But the sight that made the greatest impression on Paul was the temple of Jerusalem, the most magnificent temple in the world. The size and elaborateness of this temple astonished people the first time that they saw it. The temple was built on the site of the original temple built by King Solomon nine hundred years earlier. King Herod had built the new temple with magnificent courtyards, stone pillars sixty feet high, and wide double columns with pillars of forty feet. The temple had entrances and exits through various courtyards, nine gates in total, with porticos and impressive wide steps on either side of the main temple. From a distance, the temple shined like a silver pearl for miles and miles, like a majestic mirage.

Jerusalem was an exciting city, hosting many nationalities. It was a magnet for travelers, merchants, traders, financial lenders, and those seeking God and traditional Judaic religious training. It was also a magnet for those observing their faith. It was here in Jerusalem that Paul was able to continue his pursuit of his religious training under the tutelage of the great Pharisee Rabbi, Gamaiel. Contrary to the Gospels that portray the Pharisees as jealous, petty, and conservative observers of the Judaic faith, just the opposite was true. The Pharisees were always willing to challenge the interpretation of the Bible and to try to have a greater understanding of the laws and commandments. And they also believed in reincarnation. Paul was a devoted Pharisee even to his death. His becoming a Jewish Christian after having accepted Jeshua as his savior and spiritual guide was not in conflict with the practice of his religion.

Paul's father had given him money for expenses and to start his business career. There were many opportunities in the bustling market places of this active city for people who were creative and had the capital to take advantage of these conditions. Paul had both.

The steaming and bustling marketplace of downtown Jerusalem was located in the heart of the city. The winding narrow streets and the homes on the hillsides all led downhill to the commercial center of the city, which featured hundreds and hundreds of retail shops, restaurants, taverns, offices of money lenders, tailor shops, bakeries, shoemakers, tentmakers, artisans and artists, music houses, wine shops, public baths, and carpet and rug manufacturers. Many of these retailers and makers of goods could not afford their own shops or facilities.

It was here that Paul took advantage of his skills and his capital. He purchased stalls and shops with his money and then rented them out at attractive monthly fees, soon developing a substantial monthly cash flow. Once having established himself in this business, he then qualified as a good risk to the money lenders. From them he borrowed funds and was able to buy additional stalls and rent them out at a much higher rate of return than his monthly interest payments. In modern terms, Paul was an entrepreneur, a commercial real estate owner, and a property manager.

There were three sects of the Judaic religion in Palestine, but they practiced their faiths together in the same temples and churches, although they had different interpretations of how the Judaic religion should be observed. There were the Pharisees, the Sadducees, and the Essenes.

The Sadducees did not believe in reincarnation. In fact, they made no claims of having knowledge of what happens after death. They felt that only God knows, although they observed their religion in a conservative fashion. Even though they numbered fewer than the Pharisees, the Jewish religion today is a carryover of the beliefs of the Sadducees. Modern Judaism does not offer any position as to what happens to the soul after death.

The Essenes had two colonies in Palestine. One was located near Mount Carmel in the northwestern portion of the province of Samaria, where Jeshua studied as a child. The second colony was twenty miles east of Jerusalem near the Dead Sea, in the mountainous area known as Qumran. It was here that the Dead Sea Scrolls were found during our modern times.

The Essenes not only believed in reincarnation, but also were greatly influenced by the Eastern philosophies and religions. They also believed in astrology. There are many people today who have speculated that Jeshua spent part of his youth being taught in Tibet, India, or Nepal. I do not know if that is accurate or not. I do know that he would have been exposed to Eastern knowledge through his Essene teachings.

Lastly, the Pharisees had the largest number of members. They also were the most influential. The Council of Sanhedrin consisted of seventy men, who were appointed by members already on the council when openings became available. Two of the qualifications for being appointed to the council were the requirements to be married and to be a father. The council was made up of both Pharisees and Sadducees, with Pharisees being in the majority. The

Sanhedrin Council literally managed all of the religious activities and civil laws of the people in Jerusalem. It made all the major decisions regarding religious as well as many of the civic activities of its people. The Romans looked to the Sanhedrin Council to maintain obedience and control over the people of Jerusalem through the Roman laws. This was particularly important in obtaining the cooperation of the people in collecting taxes for Rome and in not having any uprisings against the Romans. The only reason the Romans occupied the two provinces of Judea and Samaria was to collect the monetary tribute annually from the people in Palestine to send back to Rome.

Paul was twenty-one-years old when he met Jeshua for the first time. Jeshua was twenty-three and not well known in Jerusalem. It was not unusual for religious leaders or self-proclaimed prophets to travel through the three provinces of Palestine, trying to inspire the local citizens. Paul had heard of Jeshua prior to their meeting but knew little of his background or intentions. At that first meeting, two brothers were traveling with Jeshua. They were fishermen from the Galilee area and their names were Peter and Andrew.

Paul and Jeshua became very close friends over the next ten years. But Paul never became close to those individuals who were known as Jeshua's disciples, his followers. Most of these men came from the area around the Sea of Galilee. They had been fishermen, who had lived in the cities and towns on the western shore along the Sea of Galilee, just as Jeshua had. This explains why none of the disciples came from Nazareth. And even though Mary and Joseph had come from Nazareth, Jeshua had not lived there. Nazareth was a small city located seventy miles north of Jerusalem.

Paul was not impressed with the disciples. Unlike Paul, they were not educated men, and Paul often felt that they did not understand Jeshua's teachings or Jeshua himself. Unlike their relationship with Jeshua, Paul's relationship was one-on-one, for Paul's friendship was not part of a group relationship. Because of this, the disciples also held resentment and jealousy towards Paul.

I have sometimes been asked, how was it possible that you claim that Jeshua and Paul knew each other when the Gospels say they did not? But the Gospels do not say that Jeshua and Paul did not know each other. Instead, they do not mention Paul, just as if he didn't exist. There are two reasons for this: They resented Paul, and Paul did not become active in the teachings of Jeshua until five years after Jeshua had died on the cross. The Gospels basically end shortly after the death of Jeshua.

You only have to read the letters of Paul to know that Paul had much greater knowledge of Jeshua's teachings then the other followers of Jeshua did, as well as a much more intimate relationship. Paul even wrote in his letters to the Corinthians, which theologians call his second letter, that, "Even though we have known Christ after the flesh, yet now we know him so no more." The proper translation should have been that he and the others had known Jeshua when he was alive, and, now that he was dead, they knew him in spirit. And in his first letter to the Corinthians, Paul wrote, "Have I not seen Jesus, the Lord?"

I discussed in the chapter on Jeshua why Jeshua had been arrested by the Romans, condemned by them, and put to death by them. Paul intentionally did not attend the crucifixion. Paul was in great shock as well as depression over Jeshua's crucifixion. At the time of Jeshua's death, Paul knew that Jeshua was the anointed one, the Messiah, the special son of God. He intimately knew Jeshua's teachings and messages, not only through the many, many times he had heard Jeshua speak to the masses, but mostly from the hundreds of private conversations he had had with Jeshua during those ten years since he met Jeshua, at the age of twenty-three and until he died at the age of thirty-three. Again, that is why he wrote about Jeshua's messages with so much greater knowledge in his letters than what is found in the Gospels.

After the death of Jeshua, His followers officially gathered in Bethany. They formed an organization called the Brotherhood or the Witnesses. It was only many years later, while Paul was teaching in Antioch, that the followers of Jeshua were given the name of Christians. To try to create credibility for their new organization, the apostles appointed Jeshua's brother, James, to become the figurehead president of the new organization. In reality, Peter was the leader of this group.

Following the death of Jeshua, the disciples, according to the Gospels, became instilled with the Holy Spirit. As a child growing up in a Catholic community, when I heard my friends speak of the Holy Spirit, I had a vision of some sort of mystical vapor or etheric gas being inside of their body. But I was wrong.

Being instilled with the Holy Spirit means having the knowledge of God's will, having the understanding of God's intentions, being committed to living your life manifesting God through your actions and behavior. That is what was meant by having the Holy Spirit.

After Jeshua's death, the disciples were no longer pupils, because they had lost their teacher. Instead, they were now called the apostles, which comes from the ancient words apostulus, which means teacher. But, contrary to what most people are taught, there were not twelve apostles. They originally numbered seventy, which was copied from the seventy-member Council of the Sanhedrin. A number of these apostles were also women. The Brotherhood accepted the practice of baptism as a ritual for those who committed to have Jeshua be the spiritual guide between themselves and God. You must understand that in Jeshua's teachings two thousand years ago, he offered himself as the spiritual leader to anybody who chose to have him. He never, never claimed that he was God. Instead, he said he was the son of God, as are every one of us the sons and daughters of God. And in so being, he said we are all part of God. In fact, in the Gospel of John, Jeshua said to his listeners, "Ye are all gods."

It is written in the Scriptures that Paul persecuted the Jews who had accepted the teachings of Jeshua. This is false. It is absolutely not true. This falsehood not only appears in the Scriptures, but also in one of Paul's letters, and it bothers me greatly. Paul never persecuted the Jews, or anybody else for that matter. He was not in a position to persecute anybody. He held no position of authority. He was not a member of any government agency or organization that would have given him the power to persecute anybody. Nor did he have any desire to.

But he was critical of the new organization. And whenever you see the word persecute in the scriptures, you should substitute the word criticize in its place. Paul did criticize the Brotherhood, or Witnesses if you prefer, during those early years following the death of Jeshua, and he was justified in doing so. The witnesses had formed a commune in Bethany, and they instructed the people who had accepted Jeshua as their spiritual guide, as well as those that they were recruiting, that in accepting Jeshua they had to give up to the organization all their worldly possessions. They were told that, if they did not do so, God would punish them. And Paul felt this was wrong. Paul had never heard Jeshua say that people had to give away one hundred percent of all their wealth, and he felt it was wrong to suggest that God was capable of punishing them. The apostles wanted the wealth for their own organization's needs, and it had nothing to do with God. Paul was critical of them for using God's name to threaten people.

Also, the apostles were recruiting pagans to accept Jeshua as their spiritual guide. But in accepting Jeshua, they also had to accept Judaism. This required the male converts to be circumcised and for all these people thereafter to only eat foods approved under Judaic law. Paul felt many of these persons were pretending to accept Jeshua and were converting to Judaism only so they could join the commune and enjoy the benefits of the wealth that had come into the organization, to be able to receive free food, shelter, and clothing.

And Paul felt that this was wrong, and he was critical, for he knew many of these people were not sincere. But he could not, and did not, persecute them.

Five years after the death of Jeshua, Paul decided to make a business trip to Damascus. His business activities had now expanded into the country of Syria. The route that Paul took from Jerusalem to Damascus was to cross the southern fork of the Jordan River at Bethany, going northeast towards Jericho, and then north through Peraea and Batanaea, a distance of one hundred and forty miles. It was a difficult and long trip through the hot arid desert. Paul did not travel this route by himself. Instead, he booked passage with a caravan, which for a fee provided security, food, water, and a camel for transportation.

At that time, you had to pay a toll at the gates before entering Damascus. The gates were closed at night time because of the lack of illumination. You would then have to camp in the desert by the roadside, waiting for sunrise, to pay the toll and pass through the gates. The village of Kakae lay ten miles southwest of Damascus. When Paul and the caravan arrived at night at Kakae, they bathed and ate, and then proceeded to Damascus, setting up their camp approximately two miles from the gate to wait for daybreak. What happened next was the most important event in Paul's life. Luke claims in the Scriptures that Paul was riding a horse that was hit by a bolt of lightning, throwing him off his horse, and that Jeshua appeared before him. That is not true. It is a fabrication of Luke's. You do not travel one hundred and forty miles through the desert on a horse.

Paul was asleep at the camp site and was awakened in the middle of the night. I have jokingly suggested at my symposiums that it may have been at 4:44 in the morning—and perhaps it was. When Paul was awakened, he felt compelled to go further into the desert, away from the campsite and from the other people. It was then that Jeshua appeared before Paul, surrounded by a brilliant light. And it is true that the light was so bright that Paul was temporarily blinded.

Jeshua talked to Paul and told him how much he loved him. He told Paul that he understood Paul's frustrations and criticisms of the apostles, but he asked Paul to overlook their faults and to help them spread Jeshua's messages throughout Palestine and the rest of the world. That was an offer that God was making to Paul, through Jeshua. And it was Paul's option, through his free will, to decline or accept this offer.

Paul accepted the offer and made a commitment to Jeshua that he would spend the rest of his life teaching the messages of Jeshua. Luke and the pre-medieval church described this event as Paul's conversion. For sixteen hundred years, the Church has preached and taught that Paul made a conversion at this important moment in history. But a conversion to what? Did Paul give up his Jewish faith in order to become a Christian? Christianity did not yet exist. Paul was to be the founder of Christianity five years later. There was nothing to convert to.

There was only one religion at that time in that part of the world. It was Judaism, and some of the Jewish people had accepted Jeshua as the Messiah, as a spiritual guide, and some had not. But it was not a conversion, it was a commitment. As you probably know, Paul made many journeys in his lifetime after the commitment. When Julia Ingram asked me when I had been regressed into the memory of Paul, what was the most important journey I had taken, I answered, "My journey to Damascus."

Paul stayed in Damascus for a while, preaching in the Jewish temples in the city. He wanted to practice the words he was to speak the rest of his life, before he returned to Jerusalem. Upon his return, he immediately went to the headquarters of the Witnesses in Bethany and told them of his commitment to help them by becoming an apostle. They were ecstatic, and, in response to his decision, they began to call him Paul, rather than Saul. It was to commemorate his important decision. Actually, his real Roman birth name was Paullus. Paul was thirty-six years old when these events took place.

Paul stayed in Judea, preaching for the next several years. He then concluded that it was in the best interests of their mission for the apostles to travel to other regions outside of Jerusalem, not only within Palestine, but also outside of the country. The apostles scattered in different directions, Peter going to Caesaria, Philip going to Samaria, and Paul sending his friend Lucius to Laodicia. Paul had evolved into a major position of leadership, and he himself left for his first mission from Jerusalem to Antioch, which at that time was a splendid city, the capitol of its country, ranking only after Rome and Alexandria. Today it is a poor town of twelve thousand people located within the country of Turkey.

The people of Antioch were known for their wit and for having a great sense of humor. They also loved to create nicknames, such as calling the emperor the goat, because of his long beard. It was here in Antioch, approximately nine years after Jeshua had died on the cross, that the people named the Brotherhood the Christians, in jest of Paul's teachings in their city.

Paul preached in Antioch for one year. So, at the age of forty-one Paul began his first journey. After leaving Palestine, he traveled to many places, some that no longer exist. He went to the Cyprus Island cities of Salamis and Paphos, to Attalia, Perga, to the region of Pisidia, to Iconium, Lystra, and Derbe and back again the same way he had come, until he again reached Antioch.

It was during this first mission that Paul realized that many of the heathens, those who had no religion or who prayed to pagan idols, could become prospects for the teachings of Jeshua and God in addition to the Jews. When Paul returned to Jerusalem to meet with the other leaders of the apostles, this became a major issue. Should they allow heathens the right to accept Jeshua as their spiritual guide to God?

Some of the apostles, including Jeshua's brother James, were adamant that, if pagans did decide to become Christians, they must accept and learn the Judaic religion, be circumcised, and agree to eat only food consistent with the dietary laws of the Jewish faith. Other apostles believed that it was more important to allow the heathens to accept Jeshua and the concept of God, even if they chose not to be circumcised and not to accept Judaism.

After several years of serious debate and arguments, it was finally decided that pagans could become Christians without embracing Judaism. Paul was now prepared to begin his second mission, at the age of forty-six, six years after he had started his first mission. His first mission had lasted over three years. He then spent another three years in Jerusalem during the great debates, and he was now to spend another three years of his life on his second mission.

But now Paul was on much more dangerous ground. No longer was he confining himself to preach to the small Jewish populations in these foreign countries, asking them to accept Jeshua as their spiritual guide. Now he was preaching to large crowds of heathens, trying to persuade them to give up their pagan practices and accept the concept of one God, and that Jeshua would be the spiritual guide to God. This created tremendous conflicts in many places for Paul. In many cases, it would break up families, marriages, alliances, friendships; children abandoned their family culture and practices that were enjoyed for generations; husbands and wives argued over the merits and disadvantages of this new belief. Paul converted many pagans to Christianity. He also exposed himself many times to anger, hostility, and danger.

It was during this time that Paul made some very important decisions that are still affecting our world today. As Paul went to one region after another, he would leave one or more of his apostles behind to become ministers and administrators of his newly found churches. His new church leaders, both men and women, were charismatic, filled with enthusiasm and looked up to by the new followers who had converted to Christianity. Unfortunately, Paul found that in too many cases his ministers had developed carnal relationships with the local people, even though in some cases his ministers were married. Also, in some cases, the local people who became involved with them were also married. This oftentimes created scandals, not unlike the scandals that we read and hear about in our own contemporary times.

So Paul made some decisions. He declared from that time on that, if ministers were married, they must have fidelity to their spouses. Infidelity would not be tolerated. And if they were not married, the single ministers would pledge to be celibate. Should they fall in love and have need for a carnal relationship, he insisted that they should marry rather than being involved sexually with another, which could cause embarrassment and defeat the purpose of their missions.

Approximately three hundred and fifty years later, the early Roman church declared that their clergy could not marry. They claimed that these were the rules established by Paul, and they were continuing to abide by them. But they were not the rules of Paul. Paul said they had to be celibate if they were not married, but they had permission to get married, if they so desired. In truth, the early Roman church adopted these practices because the church had tremendous wealth. They feared that, if the clergy married, when they died they would leave their wealth to their wives and children rather than to the church. That was the reason they would not allow those of the cloth to get married, not because Paul had made that decision, which he had not. In reality, the pre-medieval church leaders were notorious for the number of mistresses they had, even though they had no wives.

Regarding the issue of women, Paul had been unfairly blamed for sixteen hundred years of being prejudiced against women. It is not true. Many women were involved in Paul's ministry every place he went. In fact, if you read the last paragraph of his letters, you will find in every case he thanks his administrators and key people in each city he writes to, and you will see the names of almost as many women as you will see of men. The decision to create a fraternity exclusively of men, in essence, "an all boy's club," was made by the church leaders of the fourth and fifth century and by their successors, not by Paul.

Following the decision to allow heathens to become Christians, Paul began his second mission. In addition to visiting places he had already been, he also went across the sea to Greece. In Greece, he converted many pagans and founded the churches in Neopolus, Phillipi, Appolonia, Thessalonika, Athens, and Corinth. He then went into Ephesus and many other places and eventually returned to Palestine. Paul was now preaching to heathens as well as to Jews. In spite of the hostility and anger caused by his efforts, and at times being physically attacked and thrown into prison, he was rewarded with substantial success. Now there existed in the world, not only Jewish Christians, but also Gentile Christians. He completed this mission at the age of forty-nine.

History claims Paul took two more journeys before he ran into serious problems in Jerusalem, at the age of fifty-eight, upon the return from his fourth mission. Paul did not think of his journeys or excursions in terms of numbers. Many times he would spend over a year in one place before going to another location. Now he was back in Jerusalem, taking time to replenish his energy and to reacquaint himself with his old friends.

Paul's position on many important subjects had changed dramatically in the twenty-three years since he had his experience on the road to Damascus. In Paul's mind there were now two branches of the Judaic religion—those who had accepted Jeshua and those who had not. But they still had only one God, our Beloved Lord.

Paul and the apostles had persuaded many, many pagans to accept Jeshua as their spiritual guide as well as to accept God as the divine creator. Even though these new Gentile Christians were not Jews, Paul had the same respect and love for them that he had for the Jewish Christians. And that is why Paul made a great error that almost cost him his life.

One of the absolute religious laws that existed in Jerusalem at that time was that those who were not of the Jewish faith were not allowed inside the Holy Temple. It would have been an act of blasphemy, an affront against God, for a person who was a non-Jew to enter into this holy site.

But Paul had lost his perspective on this issue. Is there not only one God? Was the temple not built to honor God? Would not one qualify to enter into the Holy Temple, provided they believed in God? And it was on this premise that Paul brought into the Holy Temple individuals who had become Gentile Christians, who were non-Jews, but who still believed in our almighty Lord.

Following this action, Paul was arrested by the Jewish authorities for having committed an act of blasphemy, an act that could have cost him his life, for it was considered that serious of an offense. Only when Paul exercised his rights as a Roman citizen, to be tried by a Roman court, was his life saved.

The Romans then took Paul to Caesaria, where he was put under house arrest. He led a quiet life during this period, writing many letters to the people in the communities in which he had founded churches in various parts of Europe and Asia Minor. He was then placed on a ship by the authorities to be sent to Rome for the Romans to decide if he should be tried for the charges brought against him in Jerusalem.

When Paul arrived in Rome, the only restriction placed on him was that he could no longer travel outside of Rome. The city was built on seven large hills, and Paul moved into a small house with a pleasant yard on one of the hillsides. He wrote many letters the last few years of his life, sometimes in his own handwriting, but most often dictating his thoughts to others, to write on his behalf, when his eyesight prevented him from doing his own writing. This is why some of the letters from the Scriptures have been attributed to him but are actually not his writings. They may have been his thoughts and ideas, but they were the words and wordings of his secretaries, with Paul's name being given credit for the letter.

Paul had many visitors those last days of his life, when he reflected on the past, the tremendous responsibilities he had undertaken in the name of Jeshua and God, his accomplishments, and his disappointments. He was very concerned about each and every Christian community he had created and about each and every church he had founded. He reflected on the messages of Jeshua that he had committed to teach for the last twenty-seven years of his life as well as the love that he had for his beloved brother who had died on the cross thirty-two years earlier.

Paul was a product of his own time, his own society. I embrace today the same messages that Paul did two thousand years ago, messages of love and compassion and truth. Many historians describe Paul as being volatile, tempestuous, mystical, defiant, quarrelsome, confrontational—a man who was a fighter. And so he was. But he was also courageous, proud, brilliant, charismatic, loving, and compassionate, and he lived his life in truth.

The one area of his life that oftentimes made him feel critical of himself and reflective was regarding his personal desires and needs. Paul had never married, but he truly respected and loved women. Because of his constant travels, it would have been difficult for Paul to have been able to lead a normal life by taking a wife and having a family. And he often preached to others the need to remain celibate, unless they did enter into a marriage contract with their partner. This decision was based on moral issues and the culture of that day, yet he was not able to live up to those same standards himself, and it bothered him greatly. That was what Paul referred to in his letters, when he spoke of "weakness of his flesh" and the "thorn in his side," not that he was a dwarf or a hunchback as some historians have ridiculously speculated.

There is a passage that Paul wrote in his letter to the Romans that the theologians never mention and that I find incredible. Perhaps it is because of the poor translation into English, or perhaps because they do not understand it, or perhaps because it makes reference to reincarnation and they do not want to acknowledge it. It is found in the middle of his long letter to the Romans, which today has been labeled as chapter seven, and I shall paraphrase for you what Paul wrote almost two thousand years.

He said there was a time in his life when he coveted, but it was not a sin because it was before the law, before the ten commandments (before the time of Moses). But then he had died, and now (in his present life), when he does covet, it is a sin because he is violating one of the ten commandments.

I will now quote to you verbatim what Paul then continued to write in his letter to the Romans. (It is identified today as Romans 7:16-24.)

> *What I do, I do not understand. For I do not do what I want, but I do what I hate. For I know that good does not dwell in me, that is, in my flesh. For I do not the*

> *good that I want to, but I do the evil I do not want to do. I see in my members another principle at war with my mind, taking me captive to the law of sin to dwell in my members, miserable one that I am. [He is talking about his sexual needs.] Who would deliver me from this mortal body?*

I have now shared the truth of Paul's anguish and guilt, the meaning of his "weakness of the flesh" and of the "thorn in his side." Some fundamentalists get frustrated at me when they hear me say this, accusing me of speaking falsely and degrading Paul, the man whom I love, as I love myself. Can they not read? Are they so blinded by the monster Fear, that they cannot read Paul's own words and accept the fact that he was a human, a dynamic, virile man with normal human needs? Paul never thought of himself as a saint, and he did not ask to be given sainthood. Paul knew who he was, and he acknowledged his weaknesses as well as his strengths.

Paul died a peaceful, comfortable death at the age of sixty-two. Based on the life he lived, the hardships he endured, the time of his life, it would have been the equivalent today of a man in his late seventies. Some theologians argue with me that he died at the hands of the Romans, that he was beheaded.

This is not true. Would a Roman citizen be put to death in Rome for bringing Gentile Christians into a Jewish temple five years earlier, in the city of Jerusalem? It is absurd. It was only shortly after his death that the Romans destroyed and tore down this very same temple. They could not have cared less what Paul did in the temple or about the crime he had been accused of in Jerusalem. Some theologians tell me I am wrong and ask me, since they have no proof that he was beheaded by the Romans, what proof can I show them that he did die a natural death. In the absence of proof, perhaps logic should dictate.

Two thousand years ago God made an offer to Paul, through Jeshua, to become a messenger for God. He made a commitment to spend the rest of his life teaching the messages to others, to help people understand their relationship with God, to offer them Jeshua as their spiritual guide, and to help them enhance their own spirituality. Paul accepted that offer and made a contract with God. Paul honored and completed that commitment. Paul's commitment rings with a tremendous similarity to what I have been told by spirit is my responsibility. Paul wrote two thousand years ago in his second letter to the Corinthians, "Entrusted to us are messages of reconciliation. So we are the ambassadors for Jeshua as if God was appealing through us."

Chapter
- 10 -
The Bible

I recently read that one of the fundamentalist religious leaders in the United States claimed the Bible was written by forty individuals. This surprised me greatly. Not that he claimed that the Bible was written by forty different people, or thirty-five or forty-five, but that he acknowledged that it was written by people at all.

I shared with you in *The Messengers* that "spirit" told me there are some people who will not accept our messages at first, and some who will never accept our messages. "Spirit" said it was because they do not have the proper spiritual DNA. I have since been asked over a hundred times: What did they mean by "spiritual DNA?"

Remember when my colleague wrote his five pages of material to me a day and a half after my first angelic experience, when he was awakened at 4:44 in the morning? The angels had written through him that some people will have difficulty accepting God's messages, because they do not have the proper DNA.

What I have since been told is that the mind is the gatekeeper of the heart and soul. Millions of people throughout the world have now opened their gates and are allowing information to come into their hearts and souls that otherwise they would not receive.

But there are those whose gates still remain closed. There are those whose closet doors are firmly shut, and they are determined not to allow the monster Fear, to be released. This is what is meant by not having the right spiritual DNA. Unfortunately, many of these people also have been taught to believe that the Bible was not written by man but was written by God. Or at least that God inspired every word of the Bible, and that the words of the Bible represent infinite truth.

They believe that the Bible must never be challenged, never questioned, and that those that do challenge or question it, or do not accept the Bible as absolute truth, are misguided or are to be held in contempt. They believe these people are considered to be opponents of God and that they possibly are influenced by that supernatural force that the pre-medieval church created, called the devil.

My heart truly goes out to these biased individuals. They are our brothers and sisters, and I love them. I want them to have the joy of living with the knowledge that we are all children of God, that God has compassion for us and does not threaten or punish us. I want them to know that God wants us to live embraced in God's love, not embraced in fear.

I have had the opportunity to appear on talk radio shows all across the country, on the East Coast, West Coast, and in the Bible Belt. The majority of the time people have received my messages with an open mind and an open heart. But at times I have been cursed, insulted, accused of blasphemy, and even accused of being an agent of the supernatural evil force, the devil.

What are the writings of the Bible? Some parts of the Bible are the history of our human race. They talk of cultures no longer existing, of countries that ceased to be, of nations that were destroyed in warfare, of societies that have disappeared. A large part of the Bible tells us of our past—how we lived, how we perceived God, how we waged war, how we loved. And I say "We," for if you do believe in reincarnation, then you come to understand that we are, in reality, reading about ourselves.

And parts of the Bible are fables, stories that were written by unknown writers who wanted their fellow men and women to understand value systems and moral ways of life. They knew people could understand ideas and concepts through parables and anecdotes, probably never assuming that thousands of years later preachers and teachers would quote these fables and demand that we believe these as actual events that happened, or God would punish us.

God made the first man out of dust. And called him Adam. Adam was lonely, so God took out one of his ribs and created Eve. A snake persuaded Eve to persuade Adam to eat an apple. Adam disobeyed God by biting into an apple, and God punished mankind forever, for this grievous sin.

Adam and Eve had two sons. One killed the other and left to travel elsewhere, to marry and raise a family. The writer never tries to explain how this man, Cain, could take a wife and raise a family, since only his mother and father lived with him on our planet.

But the writer did not care. Even though his words were meant to be read by his contemporaries, people who were not very educated and not very sophisticated, he knew that they would understand. The story was just a fable, designed to help you understand that if we live our lives according to God's will, we will experience paradise, Gardens of Eden. Violate God's will, and you create hardship and discomfort. It never occurred to the author that millions and millions of people, thousands of years later, would be commanded by their religious teachers and preachers to believe in the story, believe that God's first creation violated God's will by being enticed by his common law wife, who was sinisterly persuaded by a snake, and that God, in anger, condemned our species for eternity.

To this day there are still people trying to locate Noah's ark in the mountains of Turkey or on the peaks of Afghanistan. An entire world was destroyed by rain, except Noah and his family, and two of every species on earth. They alone were the only survivors of the forty days of rain that flooded the earth. The ark surely had to be the largest of all the animal zoos ever in existence, although it floated and was made of wood. The food that had to be available to feed the animals surely must have required the hugest floating warehouse that ever existed. I would not have liked to have been responsible for cleaning up the cages or compartments that separated the animals. The writer who created the story of Noah would only shake his head in astonishment and disbelief, if he or she had ever been told that the ark is still being searched for today, thousands of years later.

On a radio talk show, I was being verbally attacked by a caller as a nonbeliever. I asked the gentleman if he truly believed that Jonah was swallowed by a whale, which he then lived in for several days, or was it possible that the story is a fable, trying to make a point that we should live our lives according to God's will? The voice on the other side of the phone answered with anger and contempt, "It wasn't a whale, it was a big fish."

One night I was watching the national religious channel on television. There were two couples having a conversation on the screen. These four people were discussing the Bible, quoting different passages, praising each other for their remarks, occasionally showing their approvals by "hallelujahs" and "amens." Then one of the men said, "You know, there are actually some people who don't believe that Jonah was swallowed by a whale?" The others looked with astonishment and disbelief at the speaker. Then the other man replied, "Why, I wouldn't care if it said that Jonah had instead swallowed the whale. We know it's true, because the Bible says that it's so." This response was followed by a chorus of "hallelujahs" and "amens."

It is not important whether you believe that these preachers are sincere and really believe in what they are saying. What is important is that millions of people around the country who are searching for truth hear their words and do believe them. And that is sad. Remember, the greatest lie that one can tell is to tell a lie in the name of God.

There is the story of Moses asking God for water for his people to drink, and God told him to ask a rock to provide the water. But, instead, Moses struck the rock with his staff and water flowed forth. The story continues, saying that, when Moses and his followers finally came to the promised land, Israel, after traveling through the desert for forty years, fighting wars with those that tried to oppose their efforts, Moses got punished. How dare he strike a rock with his staff. God's punishment for that act was that Moses could never set foot in Israel. Instead, his brother Aaron would lead his people into the promised land.

The moral is what? Do not waste forty years of desert wandering by striking a rock with a staff? For thousands of years religious teachers have tried to explain and interpret the reaction by God, trying to justify the banishment of Moses. Had it ever occurred to any of them to challenge the story writing and skills of the author instead?

During a talk show in Minneapolis, a caller was very angry at me. "How dare you state that the Bible was not written by God and that every word is not true?" I asked him to consider the section of the Bible called Chronicles. We are told that King David of Israel was waging many wars with other nations, as directed to do so by God. We are then told that David decided to conduct a census to determine how many men he had available for his army, and that God was angry at David for taking the census, so God brought down a plague of punishment that killed seventy thousand innocent men, women, and children who were citizens of David's kingdom.

I asked the caller, "Do you think that God would truly kill seventy thousand innocent people? Or do you think perhaps that the person writing Chronicles may have been angry at David, because he was included in the census?" The caller screamed his response at me, his voice trembling in fear and anger. "Of course, it's true that God killed those people. It says so in the Bible."

People wrote the Bible, and God was perceived to be as their needs dictated. During the period they were at war with other tribes and nations, God was a warrior God. God commanded the people into battle, sometimes providing support teams made up of sword-bearing angels. And when they lost a battle, it was usually explained to be the result of the people either saying or doing something that angered God.

There are many times in the Bible that God punishes people. He turns entire populations into pillars of salt, brings plague and disease to those who are defiant, kills innocent sons and daughters, their children, and their servants. Job is an example of one whose children were killed as a test of his faith in God.

Is that your God and my God that we are reading about? Does our God take the lives of children, innocent people on a whim, in a moment of anger, in response to a discretion? We do not have to answer that question, for there is only one God. And God, as I have discussed with you in my chapter called "God," is not a duality. God only knows love.

I've shared my belief that the Bible is the history of our people and that it also is a collection of parables that are designed to inspire us and to teach us ideals and values. It is also a collection of some of the world's greatest poetry, words of love, psalms filled with magic, beauty, and wisdom. I encourage you to read the Bible and to exercise the intelligence that God has given you to be able to distinguish the words of some of the writings that were inspired by God—writings that are parables, that teach us values and morality; writings that represent the history of mankind; and some words of individuals who are sharing their own fantasies or releasing their own anger or frustrations.

Do not be critical of those who read the Bible and choose to literally accept every word of it, as if it was written by God. That is their right, through the gift of free will that God has given to them. I cannot conceive of any harm that can come to them, if some of our brothers and sisters chose to believe that time began with just one man and one woman bearing two sons; that the world was once destroyed by a flood, with the only survivors being on an ark with all the animal species of the world; and that God sometimes is a punishing God, who occasionally acts in anger. That is their right.

But I also ask of those who choose to accept each word of the Bible literally to not be judgmental of your brothers and sisters who choose not to. Why should you have disdain or hostility to those who do not? Surely the Bible must teach you to have tolerance and love.

In all the radio talk shows I have done, when I have been verbally attacked by callers who believe in the Bible literally, I have always responded to their anger with respect and love. One night, when a caller was particularly abusive to me, I responded, "Paul said in his letters to the Romans that I shall not judge you, and that you should not judge me, for only the Lord shall judge us both. I do not take the Bible literally, but I do not judge you. Yet, you take the Bible literally and you judge me. Is not something wrong with this scenario?" The caller understood my words, and spoke more gently.

It is important that we all understand that we should respect each other's right to interpret the Bible as each of us choose to. It should never be the cause of prejudice, hostility, or the polarization of people. You should love and respect your brothers and sisters who are searching for God in words written thousands of years ago, and they, in turn, must never use words they attribute to God to create feelings of bigotry or hostility towards others.

One night, in a moment of curiosity, I found myself watching the religious channel on TV. I am always surprised by the emotions that are evoked within me at different times while watching these TV religious performances. Sometimes I find myself amused, sometimes I feel sadness, and sometimes incredulity.

Five individuals, four men and one woman, were on the screen that night, participating in animated conversations. They were discussing that the end of the world was soon going to be upon us. To justify their supposedly deep convictions, they took turns announcing their prophecies and then shouted out to each other words of encouragement such as, "Yes, yes, Revelations, chapter nine," or, "I know, I know, Revelations, chapter six."

These confirmations were provided with great enthusiasm and excitement and even appeared to be provided with enjoyment. One of the men stated that he was a good friend of a well-known author who had written a book regarding doomsday, the coming of the end of the world, and the main host responded by remarking what a great man the doomsday author was and proudly claimed that the author had been on his program several times.

Close to my reaching the saturation point of having the ability to continue listening, the host then stated, "I ask you, God, when the time comes, please take me in the first round, for I don't want to be around to see the suffering and pain." This was followed by shouts of "hallelujahs" and "amens" from his four guests. Then the camera panned on the concerned audience which applauded its religious leaders in quiet and frightened admiration.

I sat on my sofa and shook my head in disbelief. I asked myself if these people were just having fun playing with the minds of their audience, or were they fraudulent preachers using God's name to deceive people? Could they actually believe the intense fear that they were joyfully selling to their frightened followers was right to do? I do not know the answer to these questions. I only know that it is sad, it is wrong, it is immoral, and it is against the will of God.

Since there are individuals who constantly preach that the end of the world is coming and who use the Book of Revelations as their absolute source of proof, their evidence, using these written words of wisdom as their justification that doomsday will soon be upon us, perhaps it is time to explore the writings that they claim are carved in stone, the writings they use to terrorize and frighten the hearts and minds of millions of innocent "God-fearing" people. Yes, words and prophecies that induce fear rather then love and hope, the words of the Book of Revelations.

This part of the Scriptures is found in the last section of the New Testament. The author of these writings was imprisoned in a Roman penal colony on the barren rocky Greek Island of Patmos. The man's name was John, not to be confused with the apostle John who had died by this time and was buried in Ephesus. This man knew that he would never see his family again. He would die in that prison. His crime? He was a Jewish Christian.

The book was written near the end of the first century A.D., during the time of the Emperor Domitian, who was known for his brutal persecution of the Christians. The Emperor Domitian was often referred to as the Beast or the Harlot, and the city of Rome was known as the city on the seven hills, for Rome was built on seven hills. It was also known as Babylon, because of its depravity.

In reading the Book of Revelations, I sit in puzzlement, and, yes, in intellectual anger. How could any person who is old enough and educated enough to have learned to read, interpret the writings of this justifiably bitter and sad man to represent anything other than his hopes and prayers that the world was going to be punished during his lifetime? His lifetime, not nineteen hundred years later.

Even in his prologue of chapter one, the author of Revelations states "For the appointed time is near." He does not say the appointed time is nineteen hundred years away, he states it "is near."

In his grief, he wrote a poem that reads, "Every eye will see him (Jeshua), even those who pierced him." We have all learned that when Jeshua was dying on the cross, he was pierced on his side by the Roman soldiers. Are these Roman soldiers still alive today, nineteen hundred-sixty-six years after they pierced Jeshua as he was dying on the cross?

The heartbroken victim then writes about the seven communities where Paul and the other apostles founded Christian churches. He writes about events that will happen in each of these seven communities as this doomsday arrives. When was the last time you read about these seven communities? Was it perhaps just yesterday you were discussing the major events taking place in Laodicea, Thyatira, Pergamum, and Smyrna? Do they even exist today? The other three Christian communities were Philadelphia, which I believe was located somewhere in Asia Minor or eastern Europe two thousand years ago, Ephesus, and Sardis. These were the communities that were important to this man nineteen hundred years ago, that are basically unheard of in our world today.

In chapter seven he states that 144,000 people are to be the chosen holy ones who will become the special leaders after the world destruction. And who does he say are these 144,000 people? They are 12,000 men that will be chosen from each of the twelve tribes of Israel, such as the tribes of Rubin, Benjamin, Zebulam, and Issacher. Do the Jewish people of today even know which tribe they are descended from? These are the twelve tribes that existed at the time of Moses. Are the preachers and teachers of fear willing to acknowledge that the leaders of the world, after their predicted doomsday comes upon us, will be 144,000 people of the Jewish faith as opposed to being Christians? For, if they were to insist that Revelations is the word of God, then they cannot choose some words and dismiss others. They have to acknowledge that what Revelations states is that, when Jeshua returns, the only people who will not be harmed are those that are of the 144,000 chosen people from the twelve Jewish tribes who have been selected by God. Are the believers and teachers of Revelations willing to accept this?

In chapter eighteen, our imprisoned author makes reference again to the city of Rome, stating that, when the ships arrive with their cargoes of chariots and slaves, incense, myrrh, and frankincense, there will be no markets in the city for these products, for the city of Rome will have been destroyed. Are we still delivering chariots and slaves to Rome today?

There are a number of different sections of Revelations that can be cited that would show how preposterous it is of those people who claim to use Revelations as their source of information that the world is coming to an end.

I will finish my evidence with just one more statement that is made by the author at the conclusion of his writing, which is, "Do not seal up the prophetic words of this book, for the appointed time is near." Does "near" mean two thousand years later?

It is time for people who profess to be the teachers of God's messages to stop preaching their fear, their despair, their gloom, their false words in the name of God. No matter how much money they are collecting from the innocent people who believe in them, IT IS WRONG! It is not the end of the world that is coming. It is the beginning of a new world. A new world that will be filled with love and compassion, a world that together we shall make, as it is truly ordained, to be on earth as it is in heaven.

Chapter
- 11 -
Reincarnation

Two thirds of the people of the world believe in reincarnation. As a result of the changes that were made by the early Roman church in the fourth and sixth centuries, only the Western world does not believe in reincarnation. Instead, it is disbelieved, challenged, unaccepted, and in many cases, scoffed at and ridiculed.

It does not make a difference whether you believe in reincarnation or not. Should you not believe in it, the only person whom it will have an impact on is yourself. However, the impact will either be minuscule or none at all, if you are still able to live your life embracing God's will. It would be much easier to understand the laws of God, which are also the laws of nature—that which is our natural system created by God—if you at least understand reincarnation, its implication, and its impact on your spirit, your soul, and your life.

Pretend there are seven people in a room and each has separate beliefs as to what happens to us when we die and our spirit leaves our bodies. One person, who is an Eskimo, believes your spirit goes to a place where it is always cool;

another, a Samoan, believes your spirit goes to a place where it is always warm; and a Native American believes your spirit goes to a place where there are happy hunting grounds. Another believes in reincarnation, the transmigration of the soul; another believes your soul may go to either heaven or hell; another believes it may possibly go to purgatory; and, lastly, another believes there is no afterlife, but, instead, only extinction.

No matter that all seven may differ in their beliefs, if one is right and the others are wrong, all six shall have the same experience as the one who is right. I know with all my heart and soul, my intellect, my personal experiences, my memories, and from the knowledge shared with me by "spirit," that reincarnation is part of the natural system of the eternal life that was created by God.

In reality, the spirit world is a continuous revolving door into the physical world. Or, if you prefer, the physical world is a continuous revolving door into the spiritual world.

What is reincarnation? It is the system of eternal life that we are all part of. What does that mean? We are not humans, who by coincidence, have a spirit and soul. We are spirits with a soul, having a human experience. How did we arrive prepared to have the human experience?

There are four different elements that we are born with, or are exposed to, that influence who we are in this lifetime. The first comprises the genes we inherit from our biological parents. Are we tall or short? Do we have blue eyes or brown eyes? Are we shy or aggressive? These inherited factors influence who we are in many different ways.

The second element is the environment in which we grow up. Are we taught as a child to share or to be selfish? Are we given early educational training to activate the neurons in our brain, or are we left to sit in front of a TV set all day watching cartoons? Are we taught self-esteem and values as a child? Or are we a victim in our own homes, trying to survive, and perhaps even being abused?

The third element is the astral plane, the position of the planets and the heavenly bodies when we were born. I had never believed in astrology, but "spirit" has told me I am wrong. It does play a part in molding who we are, although a comparatively slight one, as compared with the other three elements. I do not want to argue the point with my brothers and sisters over the relevancy of our horoscopes. Please, know that I respect your right to believe in astrology, to whatever degree you choose.

The fourth element that influences your present life is your past-life experiences. It is the most important of all the four elements by an incredible margin. It explains why four children can be born of the same family, inheriting genes from the same parents, be raised in exactly the same environment, and yet be totally different.

One child grows up to be a scholar and an academic leader. Another drops out of school and lives a life of crime, victimizing society. The third becomes an entrepreneur, driven by a desire to accumulate wealth and material things. And the fourth becomes a spiritual leader, dedicating his or her life to help others find God. One of the four is gifted in music, another in athletics, a third is an artist, and the fourth is a scientist.

The explanation of the differences of the four children is not found in their inheriting genes from different parents, in their upbringing, or in the stars, but instead in the past experiences that their souls bring with them from their past lives. The talents and skills that have been previously developed, the needs of the soul that have been previously established, and the karmic reward and debts that are to be collected or paid for, this is what is the greatest influence on the lives of each of us.

The information I now share with you came to me by "spirit." As I explained earlier, I am not a clairvoyant who can see into the spirit world. I am not a clairaudiant, who can hear into the spiritual world. But in 1995 God gave me the gift of claircognizance, the ability to receive information from the spiritual world.

If the information I now share regarding the origin of man is inaccurate, it is because "spirit" intentionally has given me false information or that "spirit" is wrong. I know that is not the case. The spirit world is a world in which not only God resides, but so do Jeshua, Siddhartha, Krishna, Meher Baba, and all the great avatars and souls that have reached perfection and the angelic realm. God created and governs the spirit world. It knows only love and truth, and I know the information that they have provided to me and that I am sharing with you is truth.

Every one of us was created as a child of God while in the spirit world. Just as a father and mother want to have children, who are created from the life and energy of their parents, God's energy and spirit created us. We are a part of God, each of us having our own individual spirit, which is part of the spirit of God.

Prior to the time our spirits came into the physical world, the earth was filled with many species that were created by God through the natural evolution of our planet. But none of these species contained our spirits. They were living things that could not have value systems, could not distinguish right from wrong, and did not have moral codes. Their systems were designed to respond to their physical needs—to eat, to sleep, to procreate, to survive, if possible. They were the hunters and the hunted. The predators and the victims.

It was decided by God and us, God's children, that we be given the opportunity to experience the physical world, the material world. We would be given the opportunity to feel the experience of hunger and the satisfaction of satisfying our hunger, the desire for physical enjoyment of the body through our sexuality and the satisfaction of that desire. We would experience the challenges of survival, procreation, and creating a society.

We would come onto the earth as a spirit with a pure soul. Coming from spirit, having never been on earth before, we knew only love, for our souls were pure. In the spiritual world, we had never been exposed to those conditions that foster greed, jealousy, anger, hostility, selfishness, cruelty, and all those daemons, or undesirable qualities and traits of the human temperament.

We knew only love.

It was our charge, our commitment to God, that we would "make it on earth as it is in heaven." This was the contract that we entered into with God.

Because we understood and knew that the physical body of the species we would choose to inhabit was not immortal, that it would deteriorate in time, so that, when our spirits returned to God upon the death of the body we inhabited, we could not return to the spirit world permanently. We could not return to the level that our pure spirits resided in before coming onto the earth, unless our souls were as pure as they were prior to our coming into our first earth experience.

In the neighborhood where God lives there are many mansions. You can only enter the specific home in which God resides if there are no blemishes on your soul, if your soul is spotless, without stain, as it was when you left the house of the Lord. Otherwise, you shall return to earth again, to remove the stains and blemishes. This was agreed upon. This is as it is.

Many species existed on earth prior to the time our spirits came into the physical world. Collectively, as the children of God, we could choose a species that would be suitable to our purpose, "to make it on earth, as it is in heaven." And the one that we chose was agile and dexterous in body. It stood erect, on two feet, and its feet walked firmly on the soil of the earth, and its arms and hands offered dexterity. Had we chosen a different species, we would have progressed substantially differently, in the homes we eventually built, in the cities we eventually created, in our modes of transportation, in our food, and in every other aspect of our lives. But we chose Homo sapiens.

Anthropologists have now discovered the remains of fossils of the skulls of Homo erectus and found that the bones date back to a time that was contemporaneous with Homo sapiens and Neanderthals. In other words, our species did not evolve from the others. Instead, all these species lived simultaneously on our earth. What in reality happened is that Homo sapiens survived because of our spirits entering into that species and not into the other two. Our spirits provided our species many advantages over the other species, which helped tremendously in our species survival.

So it was decided by God and God's children that the next generation of newborns to the species of Homo sapiens (man) would contain within that newborn, a part of God's spirit, our spirit, which would make them God's children. And from that day on, every child born from that species would be a human in whom resided a spirit with a soul, a child of God. And it was then that the world experienced its greatest change. It was then that God's children walked the earth.

When the first generation of children grew older, they recognized that they were different than their parents. Unlike their parents, they could distinguish right from wrong, they could make moral judgments, they could feel the emotions of love and compassion or fear and hate. They could reason, plan, and create sounds to communicate between themselves. They recognized that they had options before they committed to actions, could devise methods of protecting themselves from predators, and could create tools and weapons to improve their advantages over the other species. It was not by accident that our species survived. Some anthropologists have wrongly assumed that we evolved from those that had become extinct.

What happens to our spirits and souls when our bodies no longer continue to function? When a child completes the fourth grade of school, he then takes a summer break. He plays the games of a fourth-grader and thinks the thoughts of a fourth-grader. And when he returns to school in the fall, he does not become a junior in high school, or become a senior in college, he advances to the next step of his education, the fifth grade.

And the same is true of our spirit. As we leave the earth plane into the spiritual world, we will enter the level of the spiritual world consistent with how high we had climbed the mountain, consistent with the level of our spiritual attainment on earth. Would the spirits of a Mother Theresa or a Nelson Mandela go into the same level of the spiritual world as the spirits of Adolf Hitler or the brutal emperor, Nero?

There are many different levels of the spirit world, just as there are many different grades of education in the academic world. Is there such a place as hell? You may choose any name you wish to call the lowest dimension of the spirit world. But it is not a place where those spirits are tortured and burned for eternity. God does not punish.

But in the lowest level of the spiritual world, of course, they do not have the same amenities found in the higher levels. And surely they would spend the majority of their time in preparation for their next incarnation on earth, evaluating their misdeeds, understanding the hurt and suffering they have caused, being made aware of the pain they inflicted on their brothers and sisters. And when they are ready, along with their guides, they will decide what lessons they must learn in their next life on earth, what challenges they must face, to heal the scars on their souls, to experience what metaphysical people refer to as *karma*, which is a sanskrit word which means action, the rewards and the retributions of our previous acts.

If you were a bigot in a previous lifetime in which you mistreated others of a different color of skin with hatred and prejudice, perhaps you may come back in your next life as one of that same race, so you can experience the pain of others treating you with the same prejudice. Or you may come back as an opponent against prejudice, fighting for equality and racial justice.

If you were a miser, a person who had great wealth and did not believe in generosity, you may come back in extreme poverty, so you may remove that mark from your soul. Or you may come back as a great philanthropist.

If you are a person who gave generously to others, who dedicated your life to helping others with their needs, then surely, you would come back in a situation that would enable you to enjoy the amenities in life that you had earned, that otherwise you may not have been exposed to.

Those comparisons could go on indefinitely. You are capable of envisioning your own, and yes, even in creating a scenario as to what may be your own *karma*, your own purposes in this lifetime. You may recognize scars that you are being given an opportunity to erase from your soul and the rewards that have been made available to you. Whether it be a loving relationship with a spouse, your child, or a friend, a special talent that you may have, a special appreciation of something in life that brings you great joy, you are the best judge to evaluate what your negative and your positive karma may be.

I am sometimes asked whether reincarnation includes coming back as an animal, or whether we may have been an animal in a past life. No. There is nothing more to be said about that, other than "no." The spirit of God's children has always, always, exclusively been confined to our species.

There is an interesting phenomena that takes place upon birth, as our spirits enter the baby that is being born. It is a natural system that has been created by God, as well as by all of us who are part of God, in that most people do not come upon the earth with those memories of past lives. I have a poem I have written which describes this phenomenon. I used my handwriting, my paper, my pencil, but I know it came from "spirit." I would now like to share that poem with you.

From Spirit to Birth

The moment had come to begin
As the infant made his way.
My spirit entered within the babe.
It was to be my birth day.

Where did I dwell before that moment?
What mystical garden or plane?
Why did I choose to be born again?
What did I have to gain?

There is so much I leave behind,
Understanding and love and sharing.
But now to enter a strange new world,
Was my choice made of courage and daring?

The cycle of life must go on.
It is not a matter of choice.
I know that the sound that I will hear
Of the stranger is my new mother's voice.

It is sad to leave behind
The comfort that was part of me.
To enter the new world of wonders,
Was I to be a he or a she?

I say goodbye to my guides.
You were so wise and so kind.
I know we shall meet again,
For coming to earth does not break our bind.

Slowly I depart as I enter.
Please, world, help me find my way.
Although I come unable to speak,
There is so much I want to say.

I bring with me thousands of years of wisdom,
Anguish and fear and joy.
The air is so cold and the slap so hard,
And the man says, you have a boy.

I do not remember the moment
In which my mind became a blank.
But now I must learn all over
To reject, accept, and thank.

It would be so much easier
If we knew what we knew in between.
But it is the way of life
That what we saw does not remain to be seen.

So I shall accept what I must,
And will do my best,
As I continue my journey,
For I know only perfection will end this quest.

For those who do not believe in reincarnation, and to those who ridicule the concept of reincarnation, I believe that they are wrong. If they think that the belief system of reincarnation has been confined to people who they consider as "new age" thinkers, they are mistaken. Throughout history, some of the greatest minds in the world, some of the greatest intellects in the world, understood and accepted reincarnation. They understood that the natural system of birth and death and rebirth continues until we reach the top of the mountain and do not have to come back on earth again, in a mortal body.

Pythagoras, the Greek philosopher, died five hundred years before Jeshua was born. Pythagoras not only believed in reincarnation, but claimed that he received as a gift the memory of his soul's past lives. The great philosopher Aristotle died 322 years before Jeshua was born. Aristotle, as well as his teacher Plato, believed in reincarnation. He stated in a number of different writings that the soul of man is immortal and can perform its proper functions by continuing to transmigrate into different physical bodies at different times. The great philosopher Plutarch died 120 years before Jeshua was born. He stated that every soul was ordained to wander between incarnations in the spiritual world until driven down again to earth and coupled with human bodies.

The Roman General, Julius Caesar died forty-four years before Jeshua was born. He stated, " Souls do not become extinct, but pass after death from one body to another." The Roman philosopher, Cicero died forty-three years before Jeshua was born. He stated there was strong proof of men knowing most things before birth, and, when they are children, they grasp enumerable facts with such speed as to show they are not then taking them in for the first time, but remember them and recall them from past lives. The Roman poet Virgil died nineteen years before Jeshua was born. He stated that all the souls, after they have passed away, are summoned by the divine ones again. In this way they become forgetful of their former earth life and revisit the world, willing to return again to new living bodies.

The Roman Emperor, Julian died in the year 368 A.D. Julian was a nephew of Constantine the Great, who was the first Roman emperor to embrace Christianity. Julian thought he was the reincarnation of Alexander the Great. The philosopher Thomas Huxley said, "Like the doctrine of evolution itself, that of reincarnation has its roots in the world of reality. None but very hasty thinkers will have rejected it on the ground of inherent absurdity." The humanitarian Albert Schweitzer said, "The idea of reincarnation contains a most comforting explanation of reality by means of which Indian thought surmounts difficulties which baffled the thinkers of Europe." The inventor Thomas Edison said, "The only survival after death I can perceive is to study the earth's cycle again."

The poet Walt Whitman said, "I am deathless, birth has brought us richness and variety. No doubt I had died myself ten thousands of times before." The philosopher, Thoreau said, "I lived in Judea eighteen centuries ago. As far back as I can remember, I have unconsciously referred to the experiences of a previous state of existence." The philosopher Schopenhauer said, "Were an Asiatic to ask me for a definition of Europe, I should be forced to answer him: It is that part of the world which is haunted by the incredible illusion that man was created out of nothing, and that his present birth is his first entrance into life." Dali, the world famous painter said, "I can remember verily my life as Saint John (Spanish mystic), I can remember the monastery, and I can remember many of Saint John's fellow monks." These are just a few of the great minds of the past who understood and embraced reincarnation.

And, yes, Jeshua and Paul believed in reincarnation. It was one of the most important teachings of Jeshua. All the great Christian teachers after Jeshua and Paul, such as Origen, Justin Martyr, and Saint Gregory, believed in reincarnation and taught reincarnation in their teachings until it was banned by the early Roman church in the year 553 A.D. I shall discuss these events in another chapter.

I do not share this information with you in hopes that you will accept reincarnation as a belief system in your life. I offer it to you, instead, for four reasons. First, so that you may respect the belief system of those who accept reincarnation, even though you may not. Just as I ask them to respect your belief system, should you choose to believe in heaven and hell, and should you believe that you only have one lifetime on earth.

The second reason is so that you may understand the journey I am on in this lifetime. If you understand the concepts of reincarnation, even if you do not accept it for yourself, then you have a greater appreciation for what I have experienced. As I have shared with you earlier, it does not disturb me if you do not believe that my spirit and soul lived in the apostle Paul. I truly am not trying to impress you with the information of my past life. The messages are what are important, not the messenger.

The third reason I share with you the concept of reincarnation is to give you every tool I possibly can to help accomplish my commitment to God. The commitment I made was to help my brothers and sisters understand their relationship with God and to enhance their own spirituality. I offer this information regarding reincarnation to help you achieve those goals. If the shoe fits and it is comfortable, wear it. If it does not, that is also fine. I still want to help you on your journey to reach the top of the mountain to be at one with God.

And the fourth reason I share with you the concept of reincarnation, is because I believe it is truth.

Chapter
- 12 -
Distortions

How did the messages of two thousand years ago become distorted? Why did the messages that were spoken and taught by Jeshua and Paul get changed? How did the messages of love get distorted to messages of fear, and the messages of compassion get changed to messages of guilt? How did the messages promoting tolerance get converted into doctrines and dogmas that polarize people, that instead of creating brotherly love, foster prejudice and bigotry?

Two thousand years ago the original scriptures and gospels were written in Aramaic, a language that was rich in metaphor and that was very descriptive, a language that originated among the Chaldon civilization that lived along the Euphrates River. This language was later translated into ancient Greek. There were many opportunities for errors. In many cases the translations were carried out independently of one another. They had to be scribed by hand, sometimes by groups of people working together, and oftentimes by individuals located in separate regions. These translations took many years. It was not unusual that words and phrases would have been interpreted differently by various scholars who had to make thousands and thousands of decisions with each translation.

From Greek, the scriptures were then translated into ancient Latin. Again, there were many opportunities for new decision making as well as errors. One of the frequently spoken sayings that has confused countless people throughout the ages has been the remark attributed to Jeshua in the Gospel of Matthew, in the extraordinary "Sermon on the Mount." These words were, "The meek shall inherit the earth." Millions of people in our own century, throughout the world, have been taught this remarkable phrase. "The meek shall inherit the earth."

What does it mean? How do we train ourselves and commit ourselves to live our lives as people who are meek in a world that is so competitive? Are we able to succeed and be meek at the same time? Do we really want to raise our children to be meek as opposed to being confident and forceful? And why would God reward us for being meek? What value or benefit is being accomplished by people who live their lives being meek?

The problem lies in the original translation of the meaning of the words spoken by Jeshua two thousand years ago. What Jeshua said on that hillside overlooking the Sea of Galilee to the hundreds gathered before him at that outdoor natural amphitheater was, "Those who live their lives according to God's words will inherit the earth. Those who abide by God's words will inherit the earth." That is what was spoken by Jeshua two thousand years ago.

What were the teachers and spiritual leaders of the first three centuries actually telling their followers? What are the words that we have today that represent the belief systems of those who continued the true teachings during and after the time of Jeshua and Paul, until the teachings were distorted?

One of the outstanding historians of the past was Philo, who was born in 20 B.C., and who died twenty-one years after Jeshua died on the cross. Philo was a great scholar, who lived in Alexandria, Egypt, and who was tremendously respected throughout the Mediterranean region during his lifetime. He wrote, "The air is full of souls; those who are nearest to the earth descending to be tied to mortal bodies return to other bodies, designed to live in them." It was apparent from his words, that Philo Judeaus believed in the transmigration of the souls and believed that, upon death, the souls are reborn again in new bodies.

As I have shared with you earlier, at the time of Jeshua, the Judaic religion believed in the concept of reincarnation. The greatest historian of the first several centuries was Flavius Josephus. He was born in the Holy Land four years after the death of Jeshua and lived until the year 100 A.D. During his lifetime he held many positions of responsibility in Palestine, including being the governor of the province of Galilee. In his famous book, *Antiquity of the Jews* (Book 18, chapter 1, 2), he wrote that, of the three sects of the Judaic religion, the Saducees did not know if the soul lived after death, but the Essenes and the Pharisees believed that it did. He wrote, "The Pharisees believe that their souls have an immortal vigor in them and that the virtuous shall have the power to revive and live again."

During the destruction of the holy city of Jerusalem by the Romans in 70 A.D., the Jewish warriors were tremendously outnumbered. Some, after holding out for many months against incredible odds, chose to take their own lives rather then be taken as prisoners by the Romans. Josephus wrote in his address to the Jewish soldiers, found in *Jewish War Book 3* (chapter 8, 5), "The bodies of men are indeed mortal and are created out of corruptible matter, but the soul is ever immortal. Do ye not remember that all pure spirits when they depart out of this life obtain a most holy place in heaven, and they are again sent into pure bodies, while the souls of those who have committed self-destruction are doomed to a region in the darkness."

It is not important whether you agree that he is accurate in his opinions regarding suicide. That is not what is important. What is important is the obvious and undeniable acceptance of his belief in reincarnation, a belief system that would soon be abandoned and condemned by the pre-medieval church three hundred years later.

Another great early Christian teacher, Justin Martyr, was born in 100 A.D., the same year that Josephus died. Justin Martyr, who died sixty-five years later, played a very important role in second-century Christianity. He wrote in his Dialogue with Trypho of the soul inhabiting more than one human body, and upon being reborn again, not remembering its previous experiences.

The greatest teacher of Christianity following the apostles was the brilliant scholar Origen, who was born in 185 A.D. and who died in the year 254 A.D. When Origen was seventeen, his father Leonides became a Christian and was arrested and executed. His Egyptian mother had also accepted Christianity. Among his famous writings are found the words, "Souls are introduced into a body according to what it deserves in former actions. Is it not rational that souls shall be introduced into bodies in accordance with their merits and previous deeds and that those who have used their bodies in doing the most good shall have a right to bodies endowed with qualities superior to the bodies of others?" He further states, "Every soul comes into this world strengthened by the victories or weakened by the defeats of his previous life."

In addition to the concept of reincarnation, these early Christian leaders rejoiced in the teachings of Jeshua and Paul. They extolled the doctrine of love and compassion, of living a life devoted to righteousness and commitment to God, not through fear but through love. What happened to these "teachings?" How did it come about that they were discarded, to be replaced by the messages of fear and guilt?

In the year 325 A.D. Constantine was the first Roman emperor to embrace Christianity. It was during this time of history that Constantine ruled over eighty million people, and that, throughout the balance of the fourth century, major changes were made in the teachings of Christianity. The Council of Nicaea was created in the small lakeshore town a short distance southwest of Constantinople. And it was The Nicaean Council that passed a creed creating Jeshua's divinity. They declared that Jeshua was separate from us who are created beings in that he was "begotten, not made." In other words, they claimed that he was God, as opposed to part of God residing within him as God's spirit resides in all of us.

Scholars were commissioned during this period of history, the fourth century, to translate the Gospels and Scriptures from ancient Latin into what they referred to as contemporary Latin. For twenty-five years the translators labored over the Scriptures and eliminated those portions the pre-medieval church leaders felt were in conflict with their new doctrines.

Constantine and his successor, Emperor Theodosius, who ruled from 379 to 395 A.D., and the leaders of the pre-medieval church united to create new teachings that included the philosophy that your spirit was not part of God, but instead, was created outside of God. According to this philosophy, you only had one life to live and salvation and redemption could only be achieved through the pre-medieval church. When you died, your soul either went to heaven or to hell, depending on your relationship with the church.

Yes, the dump outside the city of Jerusalem two thousand years ago that burned twenty-four hours a day became the role model for the pre-medieval church for the concept of hell. The refuse and waste area called Gehenna, in the Valley of Hinnon, had now become a location to be found underneath the earth, where souls who lived outside the rules and regulations of the pre-medieval church would be burned and punished for eternity. In the teachings of the pre-medieval church, they also created a supernatural evil power that would struggle for control of your mind against the wishes of God, unless you received the protection of the church.

Six hundred years before the birth of Jeshua, Satan was referred to as one of God's angels. In the Old Testament's The Book of Numbers, it is written that God sent down an obedient servant—a Satan angel—to help God by obstructing the pathway of the mystic Balaam, who was riding on his donkey to meet with Israel's enemies so he could place a curse on the Israeli nation. Also, in the story of Job, God told Satan about one of his loyal subjects, and Satan issued a challenge to God to put Job through a test. In the Old Testament, Satan is not depicted nor does he appear as he does today, as a leader of an evil empire. As a matter of fact, the Israeli nation, before Jeshua, was constantly at war with other nations, including the Canaanites. The Canaanites prayed to a God that they called Beelzebub. The Israelis claimed that Beelzebub was the enemy of their people and therefore an enemy of their God, our God. The pre-medieval church conveniently used the name Beelzebub as a synonym for Satan.

Two thousand years ago, Satan was used as a word of insult from one person to another, as a word of disdain. It would be equivalent to calling someone a fool, worthless, one to be held in low regard. Even in the Gospels, when Jeshua got angry at Peter, He said, "Step aside Satan." He certainly was not suggesting that Peter was the devil. Even today in the Mideast, the word Satan is used as an insult, such as the insults of Hussein of Iraq, when he speaks despairingly of the United States being the Great Satan. But the pre-medieval church felt the necessity of creating a supernatural evil force that could take control of your life in the event you had not earned the protection of the church.

Is it any wonder that reincarnation could not be tolerated by the leaders of the pre-medieval church? Under the concept of reincarnation, you are responsible for your own actions. Under the doctrine of the pre-medieval church, you could only be protected against having committed evil actions by the church. Under the concept of reincarnation, you would be rewarded by your good actions or have to make retribution for your misdeeds in your future lifetimes or during your present lifetime. Under the doctrine of the pre-medieval church, restitution and salvation could only take place underneath the umbrella of the church. Under reincarnation, God did not punish you. He was the creator of all that was loving, and you took responsibility for your own retribution. Under the teachings of the pre-medieval church, God would reward you or punish you by sending you to heaven or hell depending on how you adhered to the dogmas and doctrines of the church.

And so the monster Fear was created. But his companion, Guilt, was also invented during this same period. Allow me to introduce you to Augustine, a man who was so ingenious that they eventually made him a saint. Augustine lived during the late fourth century. This brilliant, dedicated man presented an idea to his colleagues, who were the leaders of the pre-medieval church. The idea was that they should proclaim to the populus that all are born in sin the moment they exit from their mothers' wombs and that they are condemned to go to hell for this sin. Every adult and every newborn child were destined for hell unless they became a member of the church and were baptized. Only then could they be absolved of the sin that they were born with.

His colleagues listened in astonishment. They asked Augustine how they could possibly convince people they were born in sin and that a little baby emerging out of its mother's womb was being born in sin? Augustine responded with a simple explanation. Adam committed the first sin when he ate the apple in the Garden of Eden, and we are all a product of Adam's sperm. He continued that Adam's sin corrupted the body and soul of the whole human race and that sin and death are the result of Adam's disobedience. Would God not condemn us for being an offspring of he who committed the original sin by eating the apple?

Can you imagine his colleagues' response? "Augie, this will never fly. People will never buy into that." But Augustine persisted, and twenty years later it became a doctrine of the church: You were born in sin and would go to hell if you did not receive redemption from the pre-medieval church.

But the plan had a flaw. The people decided it would be better to wait to be baptized until they were on their deathbed. If you were baptized at an early age or baptized your children at birth, would they not then be condemned to hell when they committed sins in the future? Even the Emperor Constantine would not allow himself to be baptized until he was on his deathbed twenty-five years after he had accepted Christianity.

But the pre-medieval church found a solution to this objection. Allow yourself to be baptized now. Regardless of how much you sinned in the future in your lifetime, the church could still proceed in giving you redemption on your deathbed, giving you a one-way ticket to heaven upon your death, regardless of what sins you had committed after your baptism. And thus, was created the cousin of the monster Fear, the concept of Guilt through original sin.

The scholars who were commissioned to translate the New Testament from ancient Latin into contemporary Latin labored for over twenty-five years. And they were instructed to purge everything dealing with reincarnation out of the Bible. One life, and that is it. It was up to you. Did you want to go to heaven or hell? Did you want the protection of the pre-medieval church, or did you want to be influenced by the evil force and have your soul burn in hell for eternity?

The church would help you live with the guilt of being responsible for the death of Jeshua and of your being born as a sinner. Is it no wonder that reincarnation was a threat to the pre-medieval church?

But even though the scholars were told to purge everything dealing with reincarnation out of the Gospels, they missed it in fifteen places. Is it not written in both the Gospels of Mark and Matthew that the disciples asked Jesus if the man standing before them who had been blind since birth, had been born blind as a punishment for his previous sins? Jeshua answered he had not been born blind for his previous sins. But surely they would have not asked that question if they had not believed in reincarnation.

And in the Gospel of Matthew, Jeshua arrives in Caesaria and asks his disciples who the people were saying that he was. They answered him that some thought he had previously been the prophet Jeremiah, and others thought he was the prophet Elijah. But Jeshua told them that he who was the prophet Elijah had already come and they had taken his life just as surely someday they would take his. And the Gospel continues to say that the disciples knew that he was talking about John the Baptist, who had already been executed.

I told this story during a Seattle radio talk show that I was featured on one afternoon. The caller, a man named David, said, "Nick, you don't know what you are talking about." He continued, "It is true that the Gospels say that John the Baptist was previously the prophet Elijah, but Nick, Elijah never died. He lived hundreds of years earlier, but he never died. He ascended to heaven. So, see, it has nothing to do with reincarnation. He ascended to heaven."

And I answered, "I see. So when his mother Elizabeth, who was a sister of Jeshua's mother, gave birth to little John, out of her womb came a 165 pound man who was fifty-six-years old. Is that correct?" David responded, "Well, no, uh, it was the spirit of Elijah that was in the body. That's it. It was the spirit of Elijah." And I said, "David, you just described reincarnation." There was a pause and then you could hear the click of the phone hanging up.

Yes, there is no question that reincarnation can be found in the New Testament as I have mentioned in earlier chapters. Paul referred to it twice in his letters to the Romans, and Jeshua referred to his own past life in the Gospel of John.

The early Christian teachers, however, did not immediately discard the concept of reincarnation in their teachings. In the fourth century, the great scholar St. Gregory wrote, "It is absolutely necessary that the soul shall be healed and purified, and, if it does not take place during this life, then it must be accomplished in future lives."

But a decision was made in the year 553 A.D. to take drastic steps to put a final and absolute stop to the teachings of reincarnation. Under the powerful control and leadership of the Emperor Justinian, the Fifth Ecumenical Council of Constantinople was called together on May 5, 553 A.D., and held meetings at Hagia Sophia. The council was presided over by Eutychius, who was the leader of the Eastern medieval church, because Pope Vigilius and forty-two percent of the bishops boycotted the hearings. Of the 165 bishops who attended, 159 were from the Eastern church, which was controlled by the emperor.

And it was during these council hearings, which were concluded one month later on June 2nd, that they passed the infamous fifteen Anathemas. Anathema was a Latin word meaning "a curse upon you." The first anathema passed was that, if anyone continued to teach the pre-existence of the soul, they would be excommunicated from the church and there would be a curse upon them. The ruling read, "If anyone assert the fabulous pre-existence of the souls, and shall assert monstrous restoration which follows from it, let him be anathema."

Even in the Old Testament there was discussion of reincarnation. In Jeremiah, chapter 1, verse 5, it states that the

Lord told Jeremiah the following: "The word of the Lord came to me thus; 'before I formed you in the womb I knew you. Before you were born I dedicated you, a prophet to the nations I appointed you.'" It is obvious that these words are referring to reincarnation, for otherwise it would not be stating God knew him before he was in the womb as well as before he was born, meaning when Jeremiah was in spirit before he was conceived in the womb. This writing took place in 650 B.C. in the small village of Anathoth, near Jerusalem.

And what did the distortions of the teachings of Jeshua and Paul bring the world? What were the ramifications of a religious doctrine that taught a belief system of one lifetime, with control placed exclusively in the hands of the leaders of the medieval church? Did they not bring to the world, during the years 1097 to 1270, two hundred years of murder, rape, plunder, and torture under the guise of religious righteousness? How many innocent lives were taken during those infamous years of the Crusades?

And you cannot help but shake your head in sadness when you think of the thousands of innocent people who were tortured and burned in the name of our beloved brother and our Lord during the Inquisition, which followed the Crusades. "Forgive them father, for they know not what they do."

And then we have the most horrible period of history during our own century, when millions of innocent people, including women and children, were mercilessly killed in concentration camps. Their crime? They had a different religion from those of their killers.

And even today, as I write these words, in Africa, in Indonesia, in Eastern Europe, in South America, in the Mideast, our brothers and sisters are being killed because of the polarization of the children of God, through the failures of the religious teachings.

Again, it truly is not important whether or not you believe in reincarnation. What is important is the damaging alternative we have been offered as a substitute to reincarnation. The belief in a punishing God; the belief in a supernatural evil force that is competing with God for your will and your mind; the belief that, if the devil succeeds, you will be condemned to live and be tortured for eternity in a place called hell; the belief that you should carry the guilt and responsibility on your shoulders that our beloved brother died on the cross two thousand years ago because of your sins; the belief that you and your children are born in sin.

It is wrong that sixteen hundred years after the monster Fear, and his cousin, Guilt, were created by the medieval church, that you and your children are still being preached to and taught by some individuals that you should live your lives in fear, rather than embracing love and compassion.

I believe that your body is a temple of God. I believe, literally, that God resides within you. I cannot be more emphatic in sharing that belief with you. And I believe that you can pray anywhere you choose, anytime you choose, for is not your temple always with you? You can pray in bed in the morning, at school or at work during the day, while you walk across a field or ride a bus, on a crowded street, or in the solitude of your own home. Your body is your temple. It is open twenty-four hours a day, to honor, acknowledge, and recognize God.

But I also believe that the church plays a very important part in many people's lives. It gives them direction, guidance, a sense of purpose, and communal worship, which is needed by many people. I encourage you to attend church services. Take your temple into a house built to honor God. A temple inside of a temple. What could be more meaningful? If you presently do not have a church, experiment. Visit four or five different churches. Attend their services until you find one that you can identify with, that gives you comfort.

But I share with you my brothers and sisters that it is time for the religious leaders of the world to step forth and tell their followers the truth. It is time for them to have the courage to acknowledge what took place both sixteen hundred years ago and fourteen hundred and fifty years ago, and to tell their followers how the messages of love got changed to messages of fear, how the messages of compassion got converted to messages of guilt, how the messages of tolerance got distorted to polarize people and to breed prejudice and bigotry.

I believe with all my heart and soul, that millions of people throughout the world, upon hearing the truth, would revere and applaud their religious leaders and will embrace them with love and respect, rather than in anger for what they have been taught all these years.

Yes, it will take tremendous courage on the part of the religious leaders of the world, courage to take the risk involved after all the years of teaching the distortions, to speak in God's truth. If they do not, they will lose their followers as we enter into the new millennium. And that is also in God's truth.

Chapter
- 13 -

Creating Love

Controlling Anger

Hundreds of books have been written on how to improve our health—no, probably thousands. We are told about what foods to eat, what foods not to eat, what exercises we should do, the fresh air we should breath, the sunshine we should avoid, and the rest and sleep that our bodies need for us to enjoy life.

But what about our souls? What can be done for our souls in order to nurture them? What can we do in our lives, by our own actions, by our own thoughts, by our own attitudes and belief systems that can nurture our souls?

During a large part of my life, I harbored anger toward others, individuals who had taken advantage of my friendship or who had defrauded or cheated me in business transactions. A number of times this anger even turned into hatred, and I harbored it inside of me. Sometimes I would lay in bed at night, into the early hours of the morning, feeling the animosity and anger I had towards those individuals, thinking how I could have used those funds to provide for my own family or for others to better their lives, rather than the money having been used by dishonest people who lacked morals and ethics. I would fantasize about getting my revenge in the courtroom and sometimes about other methods of retribution. In the last several years I was taught by "spirit" that having this anger inside of me was interfering with my ability to have harmony, peace, and happiness and being at one with that part inside of me that is God, as well as enhancing my own spirituality.

Having that anger fermenting within me was not hurting those individuals. It was hurting me. It was not only affecting my sleep, it was affecting my attitude, the peace and harmony I had a right to enjoy, and my behavior towards the many people in my life who I loved and respected.

And just as I have come to understand that the mind is truly the gatekeeper to your heart and soul, that it can prevent negative thoughts and feelings from going into your heart and soul by stopping them at the gate, I have also discovered just the opposite is true. I have discovered that you can also open the gate to release from your heart and soul all things that are negative. You can release all the anger, all the hostilities, all the frustrations from inside of you, and instead, deal with them strictly on an intellectual level within your mind.

Having acquired that simple wisdom, I have opened this gate, and my life has never been the same. I still know that these people are dishonest and not deserving of my friendship, my respect, and my trust. But I now know this intellectually, and my heart and soul does not have the poison of anger within me any longer. I can still make intelligent decisions as to how to deal with them, but I do it without the negative emotions inside of me that were anguishing to my soul.

And you can do the same. It will change your life forever. I would first suggest to you that you take a pencil and paper, and write down the names of every person or group of people that are causing you to have anger in your heart. Write down the experiences that you have kept in your memory that are causing you to have this anger inside of you. Now, having written them down, make a commitment to God, to Jeshua if he is your spiritual guide, to your angels, and most important of all, to that part of you that is God, inside of you. Make a commitment that you are totally releasing all that anger that has accumulated inside of you. There is no longer any room in your heart for it. It has no place within you. Your heart and soul is a temple of God. Your temple is a sacred place. There is no room for garbage or negativity inside your temple. Throw them out, not only for now, but forever.

As new events happen in your life, events that in the past would have caused anger inside of you, you will be truly amazed what will then happen. You will find that you will intellectually understand and acknowledge the incident, that it will register in your mind, but your mind will not allow it to then enter into your sacred temple. You will deal with it intellectually, not emotionally. And in so doing, you will become wiser and more effective in responding to the anger and the incident. But more importantly, your heart and soul will rejoice over the absence of anger, hatred, and hostility within you.

Make a commitment to do it now. Not tomorrow, not next week, but now. God and your angels will be so grateful to you, and you will feel the joy, relief, and ecstasy immediately.

I am not suggesting to you that you will never again experience anger. Anger is a normal human emotion that we are all capable of experiencing. Even Jeshua felt anger at different times in his life. He felt anger at the activities taking place in the Holy Temple, where the money changers were converting Roman coins into shekels, which were Jewish coins. People would then take the shekels and use them to buy doves and animals to offer as sacrifices to the temple priests. Jeshua felt anger at these activities, for he felt they were wrong.

Anger is a human emotion that we all experience, but what is important is how you process that anger. Mahatma Gandhi felt anger at the treatment of his people by the English occupiers and oppressors. His anger manifested into his doctrine of nonviolence, which eventually gave independence and freedom to two hundred million of his people.

In America, Martin Luther King, Jr. used his anger to fight against the discrimination of people of his race. He also created a doctrine of nonviolence, which united both Black and White people all over the country in a common cause, and which then made a major impact on the progress of the civil rights movement.

We know of men and women throughout history and all over the world who had used their anger as a catalyst for many different important events: To win equal rights for women, to stop the abuse of children, to overthrow corrupt governments, to liberate people from slavery, and to feed the hungry. So, it is not anger that is wrong. It is what you do with that anger that might be wrong. And the thing you do not want to do is to let it turn into hatred. The thing you do not want to do is allow it to go into your hearts and souls and to have a negative effect on your sacred temple, that part inside of you that is part of God.

Controlling Frustration

I am a person who has a tremendous belief in what I refer to as fairness. It is ingrained in me. Not only do I want to be fair to others, but I also want others to be fair to me. Before gaining control of frustration, when I had been waiting in line for half an hour to get into a public event, I would feel resentment and frustration with the person who only then arrived and got ahead of me in line. When I would be driving for miles behind a long line of cars in the right-hand lane to take the next exit from the freeway, I would feel resentment and frustration toward those who would speed up alongside of me in the next lane and cut in front of me just before we got to the exit.

It wasn't really anger, for they were strangers to me. And it wasn't a personal thing toward me, for they did not know me. It was a temporary thing, as was the negative emotion that I would feel toward them. But, still, my harmony was affected, and my attitude was affected. I was very capable of expressing an obscenity, or showing my resentment by my body language or by a hand gesture. It was causing no one discomfort but myself and the companions who might be with me. I am sure you have had this happen to you many times in your daily life. And I am sure you have experienced the same frustration and resentment toward those individuals whose actions were not fair and who tried to "beat" the system.

Spirit has made me understand that we have a choice of how to deal with those circumstances in a different way, a way that actually makes our hearts sing, and our souls rejoice. Rather than shouting words that they cannot hear, expressing body language that they cannot see, "spirit" has taught me to smile instead, and to quietly say to the offender, "God bless you." Three simple words, "God bless you." Perhaps in just reading these words, in understanding this simple concept, it is bringing a slight smile to your lips at this moment.

"God bless you." It really works.

Understanding Unconditional Love

I am often asked if I believe we should have unconditional love for others? I have come to realize that I believe in unconditional love, but with certain conditions. I suppose you could refer to it as conditional unconditional love.

I believe parents should have unconditional love for their babies, their infants, their toddlers, and their young children. But I also believe that, when a child is no longer a child, but has now grown up, regardless of whose child it was, there are certain responsibilities they have to meet in order to qualify for unconditional love. In other words, all of us have certain standards we must live by if we hope to receive unconditional love from our brothers and sisters. Does God expect you to have unconditional love for a person who sexually abused your child? I think not. Are we expected to have unconditional love for those who intentionally violate God's laws and become victimizers of others? I think not.

I truly believe we are not required to allow people to be part of our lives who have negative influences on us, or who have a negative impact on our relationship with God, people who affect our ability to be at peace and in harmony with that part of us that is also part of God.

I shared this same information with the audience at my Seattle symposium in April of 1997. Shortly afterwards I received a letter from a woman in Seattle who told me the following story. She said that she had felt obligated to visit her in-laws on a regular basis, along with her husband and their two young children. Shortly after the symposium, she went to their home on a Sunday to find the typical situation of the house being filled with cigarette smoke, even though the in-laws knew that she and the children would be visiting them. Upon their arrival, they also were treated with rudeness, disrespect, and indifference.

Later that day she thought of the remarks that she and her husband had heard me speak several days earlier, and she confronted her husband. She no longer felt compelled to visit her in-laws, to subject herself and their children to the in-laws "lack of love," and he understood and agreed.

She told me how grateful she was for my giving her the words that became the catalyst to releasing her from that negativity and disharmony.

You do not have to have a relationship with people who cause you disharmony and who are affecting the peace and serenity of your souls. If it is a parent or any blood relationship who is having a negative impact on your life, give them your unconditional love at a distance, through phone calls or through the mail. You have the right to enjoy life and to refrain from personal contact with those who are violating that right.

If you were driving your car and one of your passengers constantly was causing discomfort and disharmony to you and your other passengers by their behavior, their attitude, and their insensitivity, it would be appropriate to discontinue having them as a passenger in your car as a courtesy to your other passengers and as a gift to yourself. And, as you do know, you are on a journey. Life is a journey. Just as you can dismiss the unloving disruptive passenger in your car, you also have the right to dismiss those who display similar behavior while being a part of your journey, your journey to be at one with God. You have the right to reject another, in order to be true to yourself.

People Helping People

After I complete my symposiums, I always allow time to meet with individuals in the audience who would like to have an inscription in their book or who just want to visit for a few moments. One evening following my presentation, as I visited with each individual, I suddenly found a group of three ladies standing in front of me. They had very serious looks on their faces and appeared to be distraught. They shared with me that one of the ladies had a serious problem and needed my help. She was a petite, quiet woman, appearing to be in her late forties. I could see the sadness in her eyes. I hugged her and asked her if she would write me a letter sharing with me what was the cause of her sorrow, for there was a fairly long line of people behind her. I promised her I would answer her.

Shortly afterwards I did receive a letter from her. She told me that she had confined herself to her home for the previous five years, praying to God every morning, day, and night, asking for guidance. She said that she was a single woman. Her children were now on their own and that she lived by herself. She felt insignificant, without purpose, lost. Considering how long and hard she had prayed, she said she did not understand why God had not answered her.

I wrote to her that God knows how much she loves, how much she cares, and that she is a good person. I told her that God did not want her to isolate herself any longer by staying home all day and praying. It is by helping others that you show your love for God and nurture your own spirit and soul. There are many of our brothers and sisters who need help from us, including children in orphanages who are greatly in need of receiving affection and attention from adults, since they do not have parents who can meet those needs. There are disabled children or disadvantaged children who have physical or mental deficiencies, children who need adults to teach them how to laugh, how to learn, how to walk, and who need to be fed, or who need to be read to. There are senior adults who can no longer feed themselves or bathe themselves and who need the loving care of others to attend to them. There are many programs in every city, in every community, in every state, that are desperately in need of people who are willing to volunteer their time to help our children and our brothers and sisters who are less fortunate.

I encouraged this woman to leave her home and to find an organization or group she could work with, so she could make a difference in other's lives as well as in her own life.

I explained to her that this was what God wanted her to do. She could enable others to enjoy life through her, which would also enable her to enjoy her own life, for she would receive the same that she would give to others — love, respect, kindness, compassion, and friendship.

Several months later she wrote to me thanking me for the advice. She is now involved in a program that provides her an outlet for showing her love to God and for God's children. She is now happy with her life and has found that which she was looking for. She is now receiving the love she was seeking by manifesting God's love.

I encourage you also to become involved in a program to help others. Even if you only have one hour a week to spare, you can be a big sister or big brother to a youngster who needs guidance, direction, and love. Or you can spend some quality time with an elderly person, reading to or just sharing with that person, so that they know that they are loved and are important. There are so many opportunities that are available to you to help others, but, in doing so, you also help yourself. You can become a messenger of God and nurture your own spirit and soul. You can become a manifestation of God.

Understanding Your Worthiness

Billions of dollars are spent in advertising every year by companies trying to make us feel we are inadequate, that our lives are lacking, and that we are not as good as others who can afford products and services that we do not have. We are shown beautiful-looking people using products while laughing and having the time of their lives, and we wonder why we do not have the same experience when we use those same products.

Advertisements want us to take vacations that we cannot afford and to purchase homes, automobiles, and appliances and go to events that are beyond our budgets. Television programs show us how the rich and famous live, trying to make us feel inferior and unsuccessful for not having similar lifestyles. When we are asked who we are most intrigued with, who we admire and look up to, we usually answer with the names of movie actors, athletes, politicians, or wealthy tycoons. We are taught that they are our heroes, yet we cannot match their performances, for we do not have their skills, their positions, or their resources to work with.

We are living in a society where we are constantly being exposed to pressures to want things we do not need or to need things we do not want. If we do not have them, we feel inferior, deprived, deflated, as if we have failed in our responsibilities to our loved ones. It affects how we feel about ourselves and our worthiness.

But, in reality, it is not truth. To believe that those things are important or will bring us happiness is a false illusion. These are not God's standards. These are not Jeshua's standards, and they should not be your standards.

A friend of mine, who is a Parisian, recently introduced me to a man in Miami who is worth many millions of dollars. This man was indulging himself in every type of luxury one could think of, and I found him boring, insensitive, rude, and uninteresting. At one point I said to my friend, "This man is rude to people." The Parisian answered, "But Nick, he is a very important person. Look how wealthy he is." I replied, "No, you are wealthier than he is, for would you change places with him right now and let your spirit and soul be within him and let him become you? Would you be willing right now to change lives, bodies, minds, your being." And he said no. So, I continued, "Then please don't tell me how important he is. He is not important, but you are important, for you are kind and sensitive. He is not important."

I say to you, do not judge yourself based on what you have or have not accumulated in material things, whether you are or are not in a position of power, or regarding what you have or have not achieved. Judge yourself on standards that would make God and Jeshua proud of you.

There will come a time when your spirit and soul will leave your body and you will return home to the "spirit world." Visualize yourself standing among your guides, the representatives of God, and they want to evaluate with you the life you have just lived. Do you think they are going to ask you how much money you had in your bank account? What the size of your home was? What kind of a car you drove? What labels were on your clothes? Where you went on your vacations? How high you can jump? How fast you can run? What your golf score was?

Or do you think they will ask you if you gave love to others? Did you feel compassion towards others? Did you help others who were less fortunate than you? Did you raise your children with ethics and high morals? Did you give friendship to others who needed your friendship? Did you give praise to others who needed praise? Did you send out love to your brothers and sisters who desperately were seeking love? Did you help others enjoy life through you?

Those are the things that are important to God and Jeshua and should be important to you. And those are the areas that are totally in your control, that you have the ability to incorporate in your life, that you are capable of attaining. Once you understand that, recognize it, accept it and make it part of your life, then you will realize and accept that no person is worthier than you, no person has more power than you, no person is a better achiever than you. For in the eyes of God, Jeshua, and in your own eyes, you are the best. You are number one. You are a special child of God.

My heroes in this lifetime have been Mother Theresa and Nelson Mandela—a woman who lived in poverty and a man who spent much of his adult life imprisoned. I want you to be my hero also. Do not covet illusion and false images. You are a part of God. Accept it and make God and Jeshua proud of you.

Generating Love

Love is the greatest manifestation of God one can give to another and one can receive from another. If every one of us in the world embraced love, we would not have wars, we would not have prisons, we would not have hungry children, we would not have abused women, for none of these things could exist in a world filled with love.

You can experience total love in your own personal life, for what you give to others, is what you get in return. The people who are in our lives come in many different degrees of intimacy to us, from those we live with everyday, to those who are total strangers who we may see once and then never again. Giving love to others should not be confined to one group as opposed to another. It should not be something you turn off and on, like a faucet in a sink, but rather should be an everyday, every moment part of your life. It should not only be part of you, it should be you.

Learn how to express love to others. Let others feel your love by your words, your body language, your attitude, the look in your eyes, your behavior, and your actions. Not only will you touch the lives of thousands of people, but you, yourself, will feel a greater joy and harmony inside of you than you have ever felt before.

Let us make a commitment today, at this moment in time, that you are willing to incorporate love in your life now, that you are willing to manifest God through your love for others and to let others experience God through the love that you provide to them.

Let us create four categories of people who are in our lives, in terms of intimacy, closeness, relationships, and contact. Category one would be your husband or wife, if you are married, or the male or female companion in your life, that "significant other." Also included would be your children and your parents, as well as your brothers and sisters. Write down all the names of the people who fall into category one. This could also include grandchildren if you have any, and any other relationships that are of that same degree of intimacy and closeness. Write down their names now.

Name	*Relationship*
1.	
2.	
3.	
4.	
5.	
6.	
7.	
8.	
9.	
10.	

Beginning today and for the next two days make an extraordinary effort to show love to these individuals. You may choose to tell them you have made that decision, or you may instead decide to let them figure it out for themselves. It is up to you, depending on which you feel you will be more comfortable with or which you feel would be more effective.

Starting immediately, begin to emanate love to these people. When you talk to them, do so with respect and kindness. Be sensitive in your choice of words, never using words that are critical or judgmental. Choose words that are loving and caring. Use simple expressions to show appreciation in thanking them for any help or service they provide to you. When you speak to them, make sure your words are always guided by gentleness and respect. Let them know how much you appreciate that they are in your life. When they talk to you, give them one hundred percent of your attention. Listen carefully to their words, so that they can tell that you care about them.

Express words of affection to your spouse, to your children, and to your parents. Thank your parents for helping you become who you are today. Thank your children for feeling blessed by their births. Thank your spouse or significant other for his or her companionship and for sharing their lives with you.

If one or more of the individuals who are in category one do not live in your area, call them on the phone and talk with them two days in a row, beginning tomorrow. You shall be this "new" person emanating love that you have committed to being today, and we shall refer to today and the next two days as days one, two, and three. You will consciously provide that special love to people in category one. Category two people will not be included until days four and five arrive. Obviously, the love that you are now generating to category one will filter over and be felt by everyone that you come in touch with in your life. But days one, two, and three, today being day one, are special days for those special people in category one.

There are many other things that you can do for these special people to let them know they are receiving your love. Find inexpensive, but thoughtful gifts that you can present to them. Not expensive ones, so they do not think that you are trying to buy their love, but rather gifts that are thoughtful. It may be flowers, a book that you know they would enjoy reading, a CD or tape of their favorite musical performers, or, for a child, a miniature car, or truck, or a doll. Also find a card to go with the gifts. Again, the key word is not costly, but instead, thoughtfulness. If you are sincere in your actions, truly make an effort to show your love. You will be amazed not only at how good the one receiving your love will feel, but also how good you will feel.

There are times when you slip, forget to speak with kindness, forget to use gentle loving words spoken with a gentle loving voice, but when this happens, immediately recover and correct yourself. If an apology is justified, apologize with one hundred percent sincerity. If an apology is not necessary or called for, just immediately revert back to being a person generating love, to replace your lapse and temporary let down.

The love you are showing and expressing on days one through three is not a temporary expression. It shall be who you are now and forever—a person giving and receiving love, a person manifesting God to others through your love.

The second category is the category for those people we come in contact with in our daily lives who are a very important part of our lives, but who are not in category one. It would include our closest friends, our closest neighbors, and possibly our roommates, if we are single. It would also include the people who work in our office and with whom we interact five days a week, whether it be coworkers, employees, or our employer. In category two are individuals who are important people in our lives, although they are not relatives. Include them under your new umbrella of love, beginning on days four and five. Many of them will already be experiencing your new efforts of sharing love through the love that you are emanating to category one on the first three days. For days four and five, however, you are making a special effort to include them into this new and wonderful experience.

Name	*Relationship*
1.	
2.	
3.	
4.	
5.	
6.	
7.	
8.	
9.	
10.	
11.	
12.	

Again, show your love through your voice and your choice of words, through your body language, and by your eye contact when they are talking to you. Show your love through offers to help them when they need help, by acknowledging them when they need to be acknowledged, by praising them when they need praise, by encouraging them when they need encouragement, by motivating them and inspiring them, by reassuring them, and by giving them love.

You can make a major difference in their lives. You will play a very important part in their lives once they realize what they are receiving from you. They will acknowledge this love by giving you the same back in return. They will be the beneficiary of your manifesting God, and you, in turn, will be at one with God.

The third category will include those individuals who you are not close to but who you see on a regular basis. They are your neighbors, the people you work with, your casual friends or friends of friends, the waiters and waitresses in the restaurant that you dine at on a regular basis, the people who wait on you at the grocery stores, the clothing stores, the cleaners, the medical offices. People you come in contact with on a regular basis, even though your relationship with them may be impersonal, confined more to an activity that is part of your life.

Relationship	
1. Neighbors	7. Friends of people in category one
2. Sales people	8. Relatives of people
3. Co-workers	9. Customers and/or clients
4. Restaurant employees	10.
5. Casual friends	11.
6. Friends of friends	12.

This category offers you great opportunities. In most cases, this category represents the largest group of people that we know in our lives, for there are so many. Unlike categories one and two, the people in this category could possibly number over a hundred, or in the hundreds. They are people we recognize by name or by sight, although we do not have a close personal relationship with them.

When you are providing and expressing love to these people, you will make an incredible difference in their lives, and in so doing, will make an incredible difference in your own life. Whenever you are eating in a restaurant, always ask the names of the people who are waiting on you. Call them by name when you talk to them. As you visit their place of employment on a regular basis, find out if they are married, how many children they have, where they are originally from, what are their special interests.

The people who work in the service industries are people who are oftentimes talked down to, ignored, and inappropriately treated as second-class citizens by people who are arrogant. You show your love for them by your sensitivities, by your appreciation for them, by your kindness and respect, by your showing that you care about them. You will be amazed by how much respect and love you get in return. It will bring you great joy. But most importantly, you are acknowledging to them that they are your brothers and sisters, that you recognize they are children of God, and in so doing, you are manifesting God and being at one with God.

Bring them under your umbrella of love on days six and seven. Obviously, you have begun to show them love before then, for it would be a byproduct, an overflowing of the love you are showing to categories one and two on days one through five. But on days six and seven there are no exceptions, no excuses, no, "I will show my love tomorrow." By the end of the seventh day, you will be feeling more joy and more love than you have ever before experienced in your life. God is blessing you, for you have made God, Jeshua, and your angels proud of you. You are manifesting God.

Category four is very simple to identify. The people in this category are the strangers in your life. The nameless voices you talk to on the phone, the nameless faces you see on the street. They ride the buses with you, they shop in the same stores that you do, they go to the public events that you attend, they patronize the same office buildings you visit.

You may only see them once in your life, or you may see them more often, not even being aware that you have seen them before. You do not know who they are, and they do not know you. But, still, they are your brothers and your sisters, for they are also the children of your Father and Mother. They are also children of God.

You can touch these people's lives in a different way than you can touch the lives of those in the other three categories. You can make them feel better by the patience you provide to them and by the respect you show to them. You do not care if they are dressed in the finest clothes money can buy or in tattered rags. You do not care if they are young or old, affluent or poor, what the color of their skin is, or the accent in their voices. You accept them as strangers, but you also accept them as your brothers and sisters.

You always smile at them when you make eye contact. You thank them with sincerity when they open the door for you, give you directions, answer your questions, wait on you, touch your life. You show your love for them by the kindness and respect you give to them when you open the door for them, give them directions, answer their questions, wait on them, and touch their lives.

You include these people under your umbrella of love on days eight and nine, although surely they will already be receiving your love as a result of the love that you are already providing to the other three categories on the first seven days of your commitment, since you will have become one who generates love to others.

The journey you are now on will not always be perfect. There will be times when you will slip or fall, just as does the gifted skier traversing the mountain, the marvelous singer who misses a note, the great orator who pronounces a word wrong, the wonderful actor who flubs a line. But you will get back on your feet, get back in tune, move your audience with your next choice of words, and win back your audience with your next lines. Do not feel dejected or defeated when you occasionally fall out of step with your commitment to experience God through your giving love to others. Bounce back immediately with enthusiasm. Allow your error to be short lived. Do not dwell on it. Correct it immediately, for you know how important it is for you to be manifesting God through your love for others. It will change your life forever.

Chapter
- 14 -
Answers

Since *The Messengers* was published, we have received several hundred letters a week at our offices. We encourage people to write to us, to share with us how our messages have affected their lives, as well as their own experiences as they continue on their spiritual journeys.

Many people write us asking for answers to questions that have occurred to them, or wanting greater insight into the messages we have shared with them in our book, as well as in our monthly newsletters. I have tried to address those questions in the material found in *In God's Truth.* How can others have angelic experiences? What is our relationship with God? Is the bible meant to be taken literally? How did the messages get distorted? I have addressed these and many, many other questions.

I am using this chapter to address the questions that may not have been answered in other chapters or that were only partially answered. If there is repetition in some cases, I hope that you will accept my apology. I felt some of the questions justified being answered twice, and sometimes I also may provide another perspective to the same issue or question.

The following are questions and answers my staff and I have selected:

Question: There are a number of people, some of whom claim to be psychics, who predict that there are going to be drastic earth changes, such as earthquakes, tidal waves, and damaging weather. Do you believe that this is true?

Nick: People are concerned about these prophesies of fear. They forget that God's love is like sunshine, and it is not fear that people should live with, but rather hope and anticipation of the wonderful opportunities that are before us. Regarding the earth's changes, it is true that there are changes taking place now and that there will continue to be changes in the future. But they are so subtle and so quiet and happening in such a manner that we are not consciously aware of them at any given moment. It is like the setting of the sun does not happen in a moment, but it continues to "happen" from the time the sun rises until it completes its setting. It is a process that is continuing. And so it is with the earth changes that are happening. They are also gradual. They are so gradual that you have to look at them over a longer period of time.

Question: Are these changes part of a punishment by God to those of us who live on earth?

Nick: What is important for people to understand is that what is transpiring actually began many, many years ago and is now just coming to fruition. People should not think that these changes are punishments and that they will be negatively affected by them. If a child believes there is a monster in the closet, then to that child the monster does exist. If a person believes they are going to get into an accident driving their automobile and they drive in fear, it is only a matter of time before that accident will happen to them. People create their own darkness; people create their own fears. Those who live in fear create their own monsters.

There is no supernatural evil force competing with God. Each of us, as an individual, can create our own beliefs, which then become our realities. Regarding the darkness you speak of, if you live in sunlight, you do not have to fear darkness, and darkness does not have to be a part of your life. If you live in darkness, then that is your reality and yours alone. There can also be a collective darkness, just as there is a collective spiritual consciousness that is of light.

Question: There are a lot of prophesies being made these days. How are we able to distinguish which prophesies are accurate and which are not?

Nick: People's minds have been tainted for two thousand years with false prophesies and distorted teachings. (Because of that, they are programmed to think in terms of future events, making them so important that they then make those events happen.) As a result, it affects their efforts in making it on earth as it is in heaven, or bringing heaven onto earth, which was the original intent. If people instead focus their energies on angelic events and miracles, then it will influence those events from happening and becoming realities.

People enter universities to receive an education, and if all they can think about is receiving a degree four years later, they become obsessed with the day of graduation and with receiving their degree, which will affect their ability to receive their education over those four years. This then would also have affected their ability to earn their degree. So, instead, it takes them six years to receive their degree rather than four, because their energy was not properly focused on the education that leads to the degree. What I am saying is that people can be overwhelmed and become filled with anxiety over the expectation of the event that is being prophesied, which will then affect the event happening in a more timely manner than it otherwise would. Focus on the day-to-day living, rather than on a future prophecy.

Question: In *The Messengers*, you spoke of certain positive events happening as we approach the next millennium. Can you share with us what those events are going to be?

Nick: I have been asked many times what specific events are going to happen as we approach the new millennium. I have been told by "spirit" that, if I speak of the events, they will become more important to people than what the real goals and the objectives are. The events will become the focal point of what is going to happen rather than the spirituality associated with them. I am told to allow the events to happen rather than have people focus on the events, and people will recognize that God is intervening in their lives. However, as the events do happen, they will be so obvious to everybody that they will speak for themselves. If I instead speak of the events before they happen, the focal point will be the speculation of whether or not the events will actually happen. It is not in the best interest of the people to focus on the events before they happen rather than understand that they are gifts that God is giving to us as signs.

Question: What effect will it have on me, if I am not aware of the presence of God within me that you have spoken of?

Nick: If you are not aware of God's presence through God's spirit, then how can you be at one with something that you are not aware of? What Jeshua tried to do two thousand years ago, was to have people understand their relationship with God so that they are aware that they are a part of God. They would then have a fluent understanding of how to become at one with God. That is part of the spiritual goal Jeshua was trying to help people understand and achieve when he walked on this earth.

If a person has the talent to be a great artist or to sing wonderful songs or to play wonderful music, and yet has never painted, sung a song, or picked up an instrument, these talents are unknown to them. So it was that Jeshua was trying to have people shed ignorance and have understanding of their relationship with God. And he tried to use examples in their own lives, of how much they are missing if they do not understand that they are able to accept that they are a part of God. That is why it is important for you to be aware of the presence of God that is within you.

Question: Is there any harm in our hearing teachings from others that may not be true?

Nick: Jeshua said that when you are a child you try to learn and to become educated, but if you have false teachers, then you do not learn and you do not become wise, for even though you have acquired knowledge, the knowledge is tainted.

But, if you are a child and you receive information that is truth, then your knowledge is blessed. Jeshua taught us of our relationship with God and how we can achieve oneness with God so that we, who are God's children, have true knowledge and understanding, as opposed to false knowledge. False knowledge has no value, since you are functioning in the dark rather than in the light of God. This is one of the concerns that Jeshua had with what was being taught at some of the services in the temples.

If the information is not accurate, but you are receiving it the same as if it were accurate, thinking you are hearing the words of God when you are not, then you are misled. We are the children of the Lord, and there are those who are teachers of the word of the Lord. But if they are teaching false information, or if we as students cannot distinguish what is false and what is truth, this will then cause us spiritual harm. Jeshua is a conduit of the truth of God's words to the children of God.

Question: How do we know when we are violating one of God's laws?

Nick: If you have envy or jealousy towards another, which in turn makes you act in such a manner that hurts the other, either in speech or in action, since many times thoughts motivate us to act, then you would be in violation of God's laws.

If you have a thought that is inappropriate towards another, but that thought does not create an action through physical or spoken words that hurts the other, then you should be complimented for having the ability to control your thoughts and not put them into action to hurt the other. You should bless the person to whom your bad thoughts were directed, just as God would bless you for not doing things either in words or in actions to hurt the other.

Question: What should we consider as being important in life?

Nick: Society has created false expectations and false priorities that people then cannot attain. If people do not attain them, then they feel they have failed themselves. It is very unfortunate, for the greatest reward one can have is that which comes from sharing love and compassion with others. If you give love and compassion to others, you shall receive the same in return. If you plant an onion seed in the ground, it grows an onion, and not a cabbage. If there are people who, instead, feel that living in an extremely expensive house, driving an extremely expensive car, or taking expensive vacations are the highest priority in their lives, then they are very unfortunate. For then, upon their failing to have those things, they feel like they have failed both themselves and those for whom they are responsible. It is unfortunate that they would allow their values to be poisoned and tainted by the false values that have become a part of our society.

For those people who feel unworthiness of themselves, that is their choice. Just as it is their choice to feel envy towards another, it is also their own choice to feel guilty for having that envy. If they are not comfortable, they have two choices: either they should not look upon their envy as something that triggers guilt or they should stop being envious. They have control over that. God gave us all free will. It is by choice if we wish to envy another and then feel guilty because of that envy or if we, instead, choose to not have that envy and therefore not feel guilt.

Question: What is your reaction to some people referring to others as being "new age"?

Nick: There are some people who are mainstream, who do not understand "new age" concepts. Even though spiritual consciousness is growing in numbers daily throughout the world, many of the messages are still being ignored.

However, there are now more and more people who are considered mainstream who are accepting "new age" philosophies and belief systems. My colleagues and I have made a commitment to try to be a bridge between those who are mainstream and those who are "new age." We are trying to bring people together and break down barriers, trying to be a bridge for mainstream people of the world, regardless of their religious backgrounds and faith, who do have a spiritual understanding. We want to bring together all these different groups to understand the messages of Jeshua and God and to be able to help these people who otherwise might not have ever listened and accepted these messages.

Question: How do you define words like ascension or the quickening?

Nick: I am sometimes asked my interpretation of the ascension, or resurrection, or other words of this nature. But I truly believe that ideas are better expressed in sentences rather than in coined words. For example, reduction of concepts to one word, such as those that are used in our political arenas, can cause adverse feelings to some people and fear to others; some people will laugh and others will have a lack of understanding. If one were to say to another, "I know a man who cares about feeding the hungry children of the world," I would hope people will applaud that man. But if, instead, people were to say about that same man, "I know a man who is an extreme liberal," many who would have applauded him for caring about hungry children of the world, are now turned off. It is very, very nonproductive to create labels. It is better to share what is taking place in sentences, so people understand.

Question: And how about people who have not lived a good life. Will they be punished when they die?

Nick: If a person has lived a terribly evil life and has not lived according to God's laws, and through free will has violated the lives of others by making them victims, that person will go to a level based on the person's position of spirituality. I do not believe that the place the person goes to is one that is eternal and consists of everlasting punishment, a place where there will always be burning and suffering. I certainly believe that it will not be the same environment that a person encounters who has lived life according to God's will. But the focus will not be on punishment, but rather on developing an understanding of how the person must atone for the things done in the past life that caused harm and hurt to other people.

The person who has lived a life in such a manner that others have been caused tremendous pain and suffering must learn those lessons so that, upon coming back in the next lifetime, the person experiences the same pain and suffering that had been caused to others in order to erase the marks and wounds to the person's soul that were established during that lifetime. If you wish to call that place hell, that part of the spirit world where people are trying to learn these lessons and understand how inappropriate their actions were in their past lifetimes, you may feel free to do so. But it is a totally different concept than what has been described as hell, so why not call it the cellar, or the basement, or downstairs, or the first rung of the ladder, or something that is more appropriate rather than a fictional evil place that was created by the pre-medieval church.

Question: You speak of free will as being a gift from God. Are there other examples of gifts that God has given us that you think are equally as important?

Nick: The three gifts that I feel are the most important ones God has given to us are the gifts of free will, the spirit of God within us, and the angels. We are the only species in the world with the gift of free will, which gives us the ability to live our lives according to God's messages or to choose to do otherwise. When we choose to do otherwise, other people become our victims, and we are then committing acts that could be described by others as evil. But God gave us the ability, instead, to do acts that help others enjoy life through us. This also helps us to enjoy our own lives.

Secondly, each one of us has angels that are assigned to us from the moment we enter this world. It is a gift of God. God's messengers are with us to guide us through our journey in life.

Lastly, the greatest gift of all is the gift of eternal and everlasting life we receive by having the spirit of God within us. These are three of the gifts that God has given to us.

Question: How do we go about changing the collective consciousness of people so that it is a spiritual, loving consciousness rather than one that is negative?

Nick: I believe with all my heart that all it requires initially is the effort of a small percentage of people, then it will grow and grow until more and more people become part of that collective consciousness. As an example, let me share with you the story of the many monkeys that lived on an island. I believe the island was somewhere in the South Pacific. Supposedly, there were sweet potatoes growing underneath the sand. The monkeys would dig up a sweet potato, and they would eat it. Because the sweet potato was covered with sand, the monkeys would make a grinding noise with their teeth when they ate it.

One day, one of the monkeys dropped a sweet potato into the water by accident, and the sand got washed off. When the monkey picked up the sweet potato and ate it, the monkey recognized the advantage of a washed sweet potato as opposed to one that was covered with sand. Some of the other monkeys saw this and they also began to wash their sweet potatoes before eating them.

Even though only a small percentage of the monkeys did this at first, through collective consciousness this practice spread to all the monkeys on the island. Eventually, thousands of monkeys were washing their sweet potatoes before eating them.

I am told there was another island not far from there where, even though they had never witnessed the washing of the sand off the sweet potatoes, eventually collective consciousness spread to them also, and all the monkeys in the nearby island began to wash their sweet potatoes.

I truly believe that we can begin a spiritual consciousness that can spread throughout the entire world in the same manner represented in the foregoing allegory. I have a vision of all of us beginning to pray together on the fourth Sunday of every month at 4:44 in the afternoon in every time zone in the country. Whether we are riding a bus, are in our home, or are in a stadium watching a ball game, at 4:44 in the afternoon we stop what we are doing and we say a collective prayer, such as the prayer that I am planning to use at the end of this book, a prayer that I believe was given to me by God. I believe this would create a spiritual consciousness that would spread throughout the world. From one time zone to another, this spiritual consciousness would spread like a wave. From the East Coast, across each time zone, until it arrives at the West Coast. And then it would spread across the Pacific Ocean on to the next part of the world. I truly believe that, even if as few as 10 percent of the people of our country would do this together, eventually we would have the majority of the people in the country participating with us in creating this spiritual consciousness. I am hoping we can begin on April 4, 1999, at 4:44 in the afternoon, as I discuss in the last chapter.

Question: At different times you have said one of the ways to communicate with your angels is to allow them to speak to you through your handwriting, your pen, and your paper. What are some of the things they have told you in the past that you can share with us?

Nick: One time I was dealing with wanting to have greater understanding of truth. I was trying to distinguish between absolute truth and perceived truth. They wrote the following to me one night:

"Nick, you search for truth. Man knows that inside lies all the understanding in the universe, but only he can draw upon the wealth that lies within. What he seeks he shall find. He who does not seek shall never enjoy the riches that are to be known."

"Who is talking?"

"It is I, your guide."

"Are you one of my angels?"

"The self is a being, one and the same. Love and truth is one. Those that love you, guide you."

That is just one of many, many messages they have shared with me that comes to mind. And, of course, many of the messages have been written in *The Messengers* as well as in this book. I am very grateful that they have opened up this channel to me. But it is a channel that can be opened by every one of you if you have the patience and willingness to do so.

Question: Why is it that more people do not have angelic visitations, instead of having the angels come to them in symbols, such as "444" and other nonvisual ways?

Nick: I have asked the angels that very same question. They told me that most people would not emotionally be able to handle having a visual experience. They feel it could be so traumatic that it would affect their ability to cope with life on a daily basis, because the experience would be so profound to them. Instead, they feel it is more appropriate to gently come into people's lives, such as the case of the "444" experiences, or during meditation and prayer. Therefore, very few people in the world can literally see angels, and we refer to those people as being clairvoyant.

I understand what they are saying. I believe it is possible to have a spiritual experience that is so profound that it affects your ability to function in everyday life, whether it be to hold a job, to be a parent to your child, or to handle other responsibilities of that nature. Look how many years it took for me to adjust to what I was experiencing before I was willing to go public with *The Messengers*. God is sensitive to people having such profound spiritual experiences that it would affect their lives. This is why I believe they usually come to us very gently and very slowly, so we can absorb these experiences in our lives in a positive way, rather than in such a sensational way we would not know how to cope with.

Question: Do you think of Jeshua's mission on earth as being a prophet or a teacher?

Nick: Every father and mother who has a child teaches the child, and this child will someday become a parent, and in turn, will teach his or her children. With Jeshua's teachings and his wisdom being the guiding light between God and those of us on earth, it is the same as one who carries a torch into a dark room so that others may find the way through the darkness by following the light. Jeshua's teaching is that torch, so that one does not have to stumble within that dark room, but instead finds the doorway to God.

Question: Since you, yourself, were a successful businessman, do you feel it is wrong for people to achieve things in life that bring them success and material things?

Nick: It is not wrong for people to have success and achieve material things in life. But, at the same time, these material things should never be used to polarize individuals from their brothers and sisters who are less fortunate. People should never become polarized because of material means, based on the amount of wealth that they have accumulated or not accumulated, just as they should not be polarized by their geographic boundaries, their political beliefs, and yes, even their religious beliefs. To polarize people is wrong, for it means we do not recognize there is a much greater priority and a much greater value that is truly the bonding of all people: that we should live together as one, since we have one common Father and Mother who is the Lord. We truly are all brothers and sisters.

Question: When you discuss the messages of Jeshua and Paul two thousand years ago that got distorted, at times it seems like you take it pretty emotionally. It really does bother you, doesn't it?

Nick: It really does. I do take it personally. One of the readers of *The Messengers* sent me a copy of a book written by Jane Roberts, which deals with the channeling of Seth, and directed me to special passages. The book was written over twenty years ago. In it Seth spoke, saying the spirit of Paul was very upset over the distortions of the truth over the last two thousand years and that the spirit of Paul would be incarnated again to set the record straight and bring truth back at this time. I am committed to have the true messages be received at this time and accepted.

Question: You talk of God speaking through Jeshua and making an offer to Paul while he was on his way to Damascus. Is there not a correlation between that event and what has happened to you?

Nick: Yes, that is accurate. God came to Paul through Jeshua and made an offer to him two thousand years ago, which Paul accepted. On January 14, 1995, God came to me through God's messengers, the angels, and made the same offer to me. I have accepted that offer and formed a covenant with God. The covenant is that I will also spend the rest of my life teaching the true messages of Jeshua and God, as Paul did two thousand years ago.

Question: Do you feel that mankind has not met the purposes that God intended when we were allowed to come onto earth?

Nick: God gave us tremendous power. We have the power to create life, but throughout the ages mankind has taken life. We were given the power to build cities and towns, but throughout the ages, mankind has also destroyed the cities and towns. God gave us a beautiful earth to inhabit, including pure rivers and lakes to recreate in and drink from, and throughout the ages man has polluted these lakes and streams. Why is it necessary that we must always think in terms of conquering the air, conquering the earth, conquering our lakes and streams, rather than learning how to live alongside natural resources and to maintain the beauty and quality of the spirit in which they were given to us? Now that we are approaching and will soon enter the new millennium, we have to take responsibility to use the power that God has given to us in accordance with God's will.

Question: If we attribute good things to God, do we also attribute bad things to God? Is God responsible for the things that bring us joy in life as well as responsible for the calamities that happen?

Nick: God gave us the opportunity to create a world for ourselves. It is supposed to be on earth as it is in heaven. A world full of joy and happiness. This can be accomplished through our free will. We are the only species in the world that has the gift of free will from God. God is not responsible for the hurtful things on earth that happen in our lives. Hurtful things result from our own actions, from the actions of others, or by accident.

Question: Why do you think there is so much difficulty and confusion in the world, and why do people have problems in dealing with life on a daily basis?

Nick: Visualize all of us being together in a giant classroom. In that same classroom there are children of all different grades. There are children of the first grade, fourth grade, high school, and college, all in the same classroom, trying to learn at the same time. We have one teacher, a fourth-grade teacher, giving us all instruction. Would there not be chaos and confusion in that classroom, taking into consideration the different levels of knowledge, maturity, and understanding?

The same is true of life. We have people who are leaders of the political world, the academic world, the religious world, and the commercial world, who truly are of many different levels of their own spiritual development. Some of them might be in the fourth grade of their spiritual enhancement, yet they are responsible for instructing us how to think and how to live our lives and for determining what our needs are, even though in many, many cases, we are of a much higher spiritual level than they are.

This is why we have so much corruption in the world. This is why there are so many decisions that are made that are not in the best interests of our society. This is why there is not more respect for our political leaders and why there is so much skepticism and cynicism towards leaders in other fields.

I truly believe with all my heart and soul that this will change as we enter the next millennium, as spiritual leadership prevails throughout the world. The priorities of our people will be so different from what they are now that we will no longer recognize our world as it is today. Greed will be replaced by charity, fear will be replaced by love, and selfishness will be replaced by compassion. We will live in a totally different world from the one we live in now, and it will be our responsibility to do what we originally committed to do for God when we were given the privilege to come onto earth. That responsibility is to make it on earth as it is in heaven. This shall come to be, as we enter into the next millennium.

I hope all my brothers and sisters will understand what I am sharing and that all of us will join together in trying to help others understand their relationship with God and enhance their own spirituality as we approach the Great Tomorrow.

Chapter
- 15 -

The Laws of God

Some teachers and preachers will tell you that the end of the world is coming. But that is not true.

As we approach and enter the next millennium, it is not the end of the world that is coming; it is the beginning of a new world. The leadership in the world in the next millennium will not be political leadership. It will not be military leadership, nor commercial leadership; nor academic leadership; nor will it be a religious leadership. The leadership in the world in the next millennium will be spiritual leadership. And people throughout the world will realize, recognize, and accept that we truly are all brothers and sisters. The billions and billions of dollars that are currently being spent for weapons of destruction will instead be spent to feed the hungry children on earth, to wipe out disease, and to raise the standard of living for all of God's children throughout our entire world.

God is asking each and every one of us to live our lives according to God's will, to live our lives in accordance with

God's Laws. And these are so simple, so easy to understand, and so easy to incorporate into our lives. God is asking that we live our lives embracing universal love and universal compassion and that we live in truth.

What does it mean to live our lives in truth? First, allow me to explain what it is like to not live our lives in truth. The politician who takes money from special interest groups and then tries to pass legislation to benefit that special interest group is not living life in truth. The attorney who knows his or her client is guilty, yet stands in front of a jury intentionally confusing them and distorting the facts, is not living life in truth. The leaders of the judicial system who allow this to happen are not living their lives in truth.

The representatives of our society who are using our dollars to build prisons to punish and incarcerate people and who are not spending sufficient dollars to change the environment and the conditions of disadvantaged children (with statistics showing that disadvantaged children will become the future criminals) are not living their lives in truth. The representatives of corporations that spend billions of dollars to persuade us to purchase products they know are harmful to us are not living their lives in truth. The politicians who make promises they know they will not keep, in order to persuade us to elect them to positions of power, are not living their lives in truth.

Billions of dollars each year are spent on prisons in our country. Statistics show that the majority of those who are in prison are from minority ethnic groups within our population. Statistics show that approximately 70 percent of the children who grow up under certain conditions in our society, without proper parental love and supervision, without adequate role models, without being taught self-esteem or proper value systems, are children who will grow up becoming victims. Many of them, in time, will eventually become adults who will then become victimizers. They, in turn, will commit crimes against innocent people, in many cases crimes of violence, also causing billions of dollars of losses to their victims. Why can't the leaders of our society recognize these truths? Why do not the leaders of our society have the courage to acknowledge these truths? Why can't the leaders of our society use our abundant resources to go to the root of the cause of these problems and help these young children? Why can't they acknowledge the truth, change the environment in which the children are being raised, teach the children self-esteem and value systems, and give the children the opportunity to become productive members of our society as opposed to victims who will then become victimizers?

Statistics show that a woman who does not have a high school education, is unmarried and gives birth to a child before her twentieth birthday, has a five times greater chance to see her child become a victim and to grow up to become a victimizer. Why can't we recognize these truths and make decisions that show compassion and love for all those who are affected by these inappropriate circumstances—for the unprepared mother; for the "underloved" child who becomes a victim and a future victimizer; and for the future victims of that child and the innocent brothers and sisters who are the taxpayers then charged billions of dollars for the punishment, incarceration, and management of those who become victimizers within our society? Is it because those who are in positions of responsibility are not willing to live in truth?

What is living in truth? It is caring about your brothers and sisters, so that you are living your life with integrity and honesty. It is conducting your life in such a manner that you are not benefiting yourself by taking unfair advantage of others. Living your life in truth is caring about the health and welfare of others rather than trying to capitalize on their trust and innocence. Dealing with these issues in a loving compassionate way to help our brothers and sisters who are both the victims and the future victimizers is living our lives in truth.

Living in truth is acknowledging these and many other problems within our society, problems that can be solved, if only those who are in power have the courage, will, and compassion to solve these problems. Living in truth is living your life with integrity and honesty through the decisions that we make and our actions, in having compassion and love for all of God's children, and by recognizing and acknowledging that we are all brothers and sisters.

What does it mean to live your life embracing universal love? Universal love means there are no boundaries to that love. Universal love goes beyond socio-economic boundaries. In spite of the difference in their affluence, a wealthy person has the same love for a poor person as for a wealthy person; a poor person has the same love for a wealthy person as for a poor person.

Universal love means that even if people have different views on political issues, it does not affect the love they have for one another. Universal love is color blind; it crosses racial barriers. You have the same love for another regardless of the difference of the color of their skin, the accents in their voices, or the background of their parents or grandparents. Universal love has no geographic boundaries. The love we have for a child in our own neighborhood is the same love that we have for a child in another part of the world.

I speak of universal love, not unconditional love. Universal love is who we love. Unconditional love is how we love. Universal love is a manifestation of our love for God. It is given by us to share not only with our spouses, families, and best friends, but also to those we hardly know—and, yes, even to the strangers in our lives.

Perhaps the most beautiful words describing love were written almost two thousand years ago in a letter that was sent to the Corinthians, by a man called the apostle Paul.

I do not feel Paul would mind if I plagiarized his words, words that are often quoted at wedding ceremonies around the world. Paul wrote the following in his letter to the Corinthians two thousand years ago:

If I speak in human and angelic tongues but do not have love, I am a resounding gong or a clashing cymbal. And if I have the gift of prophecy and comprehend all mysteries and all knowledge, if I have all faith so as to move mountains, but do not have love, I am nothing. If I give away everything I own, and if I hand my body over so that I may boast but I do not have love, I gain nothing.

Love is patient, love is kind. It is not jealous, love is not pompous, it is not inflated, it is not rude, it does not seek its own interest, it is not quick-tempered, it does not brood over injury, it does not rejoice over wrongdoing, but rejoices with the truth. It bears all things, believes all things, hopes all things, endures all things.

Love never fails. If there are prophecies, they will be brought to nothing; if tongues, they will cease; if knowledge, it will be brought to nothing. For we know partially and we prophesy partially, but when the perfect comes, the partial will pass away. When I was a child, I used to talk like a child, think as a child, reason as a child; when I became a man, I put aside childish things. At present we see indistinctly, as in a mirror, but then face to face. At present I know partially; then I shall know fully, as I am fully known. So faith, hope, love remain, these three; but the greatest of these is love.

1 Corinthians 13

Give to others universal love. Remember, we all are truly a mirror of ourselves. That which you receive is that which you have given in return to others. An onion seed grows an onion.

What is universal compassion? It is caring and having concern for the welfare and lives of our brothers and sisters, again, with no barriers and no boundaries. "Spirit" wants you to have compassion without attachment. There is too much suffering and hurting in the world for you to attach yourself to that suffering and hurt. We are bombarded on television, on radio, in newspapers and magazines with events and stories that require, and yes, almost demand our compassion. You must not attach yourself or adopt that pain and suffering into yourself, for our souls cannot absorb it.

Instead, let us use that concern and compassion to alleviate the suffering and hurt and pain. Let us devise solutions to feed the hungry. We have the resources and ability to do so. Let us find ways to conquer disease and poverty. God has given us our earth with all the resources we would ever need to wipe out and eliminate disease, to wipe out and eliminate poverty, to shelter the homeless, to care and provide for the disabled. Showing compassion is to acknowledge that there are those who are our brothers and sisters who need our help and for us to take action in providing help to our brothers and sisters and to the children of our brothers and sisters, to alleviate hunger, disease, poverty, pain, and suffering.

It is absolutely imperative as we approach the new millennium that we place people in positions of responsibility who do accept the laws of God, who do live their lives embracing universal love, universal compassion, and living in truth.

We should not elect people to political positions who do not embrace universal love, universal compassion, and living in truth. We should not appoint people to positions of responsibility in the academic world who do not embrace universal love, universal compassion, and living in truth. As shareholders of corporations, we should not elect people to positions of authority in the corporate world who do not live their lives embracing universal love, universal compassion, and living in truth. As employers, we should not hire people who do not live their lives embracing universal love, universal compassion, and living in truth. We should not have people as our friends who do not live their lives embracing universal love, universal compassion and living in truth.

We should not listen to or support those who claim to be the preachers and teachers of God, but yet who teach fear instead of love, who promote the polarization of our brothers and sisters, rather than acknowledge that the Lord is our Father and our Mother, that we are all God's children, and that we are all brothers and sisters.

Yes, it shall come to be within the next millennium that those who are not living their lives in accordance with the laws of God, living their lives embracing universal love, universal compassion, and living in truth, will become irrelevant to society. They will become ostracized through their own actions. It will be their choice if they are not willing to commit to changing the way they live, or if they choose instead to be a caring, loving, compassionate member of our society, living their lives in truth, as opposed to being an outsider, living outside of the laws of God.

There will be events that will happen in our world, as we enter the next millennium, that everyone on this entire globe, no matter where they live, will recognize as God intervening in our lives. There are events that will happen in the world, in which it will not matter what your religious or spiritual beliefs are, or even if a person is an agnostic or does not believe in God. They will recognize and acknowledge that God is intervening in all of our lives. They will recognize and acknowledge that miracles are happening. There will be no other explanation.

I am not talking about acts of destruction. Yes, there will be earthquakes, floods, tornadoes, and volcanos in the future. There always has been; there always will be. These are acts of nature, not acts of God. They are caused by the stress on the earth, the misuse of earth's resources, and the natural weather conditions. They have occurred throughout history and will continue to occur in the future.

There were great floods and the bubonic plague in the 1300s that took the lives of 25 percent of the population of the people in Europe. Did these events cause the end of the world? Do not honor the fear of the proponents of those who preach and teach fear by attempting to prove their point by depicting every flood and every earthquake as an intentional act of God and as evidence that we are soon to experience the end of the world.

These capitalizers on fear are not living their lives in truth. They have their own motives and their own agendas for teaching fear. It is easy to distinguish between those who teach love and those who teach fear. As a child of God, reach out and accept love, be strong and reject fear. Live your lives in accordance with the laws of God. Live your lives embracing universal love, universal compassion, and living in truth.

Chapter
- 16 -

Spiritual Healing

Two thousand years ago, one of the ways that Jeshua manifested his love was by providing spiritual healings for his brothers and sisters. Hundreds of years earlier, the great philosophers, Plato and Pythagoras, spoke of *daemons,* which were undesirable character traits possessed by people that would affect their attitudes and their behavior and would contaminate their very souls.

Jeshua knew, through the wisdom of his spiritual mind, that it was important for people to be able to acknowledge these *daemons* and to be willing to release them from their value systems, thoughts, and actions, for they were affecting their spirituality. They were causing harm to their souls, as well as to their physical bodies.

Jeshua affected the people by persuading them to release the *daemons* from their lives and to give up a life controlled by greed, jealousy, hatred, anger, fear, and all the other *daemons* that can poison our souls, hearts, and minds.

The original Aramaic words of the Gospels spoke of Jeshua ridding people of these *daemons* during his healings.

But the medieval church was not satisfied with these acts of compassion by Jeshua and changed the word *daemons* to demons. Was not more fear created in people's hearts, if they thought they were possessed with evil demons and if they now believed it was the responsibility of the medieval church to compel and demand that these demons be driven out of people's bodies and minds? People would believe that half of the population of Jerusalem was possessed by these devilish little creatures that somehow had physically manifested themselves in God's children.

In the last portion of every symposium I give, I conduct a spiritual healing. I have witnessed the tremendous spiritual energy that has taken place during this spiritual healing. I have witnessed the joy and the opening of the hearts and souls of the many hundreds of people who are in the audience as I proceeded to use the same techniques Jeshua did two thousand years ago and that Jeshua also taught Paul.

As I watch these spiritual healings take place, I literally feel that we are in a time capsule going back two thousand years. Not only have I watched hundreds and hundreds of people be spiritually healed, but I have also had others write to me afterwards, telling me that they received a physical healing as well. Also, hundreds of people in cities around the country have testified that they have seen angels standing on the stage with me while I was giving these spiritual healings.

I now ask you to join me in your own spiritual healing. I ask you to select a quiet, pleasant place to read this chapter, whether it be in your home or outdoors. I ask that you shut off all outside distractions so that you may join me in solitude and in a focused meditation. I ask that you concentrate on the words that have been given to me and that I now share with you.

I ask that you totally relax, not only your body, but also quiet your heart and your mind. Allow your mind to open up the gates, allow your thoughts to be confined to what I am sharing with you and do not allow any outside distractions to interfere with what we are now going to experience together.

This spiritual healing can make a major difference in your life. It is one that should be continual, just as your relationship with God should be ongoing. I ask that you read this chapter once each week for the next four weeks, so that it becomes a part of you, so that your soul can be cleansed and your spirit can be healed, and so that you become closer to being at one with God.

I am asking that you first pray to God and ask God's permission to participate in this spiritual healing we are going to experience together. I ask that you take sixty seconds or more, and in your own words, ask permission of God, permission of Jeshua, and permission of your loving angels that you may be the recipient of this spiritual healing and that they also help you in opening your heart and soul to these words. Please do so now, using your own words as to how you choose to ask for this permission from God, Jeshua, and your own angels. (Sixty seconds or more of prayer should have gone by before you continue.)

I am now asking for that same permission. Dear God, my loving beloved God, who is the creator of all that exists, and my loving brother Jeshua, who is my spiritual guide and who has given me greater understanding of the Lord, and my loving angels, you who are the messengers of God, I ask all of you for your permission, to allow me to proceed with the spiritual healing for my brothers and sisters. Please allow me to share your words with my brother or sister. I am also asking my Father and Mother, my brother, and those of the angelic realm, to participate with me in this spiritual healing. I ask that you surround my brother or sister with a white protective light, a light representing love and spiritual understanding, and that you help him or her in opening up their heart and soul to receive that information that will help in their spiritual growth. I thank you with all my heart and soul for the permission you are granting me in being able to share these words with my brother and sister, whom I know you love as dearly as I love them.

My dearest brother and sister, is it not true that we live in an incredible moment in time? I speak of a moment in time, not as if it were a few seconds, or a few minutes, or an hour. It can be any period of time that we choose. But this moment of time in which we are together now is such a special moment. It is a bridge between the millions and millions of years that have transpired before us and the millions and millions of years that are to come. This is a glorious moment in time, for it connects the infinite past with the infinite future. And now we are sharing this moment together.

You truly know that the spirit of God resides within you. You know with all of your heart and soul that you are a child of God. You know that the Lord is your Father and Mother and that the greatest gift that your Father and Mother has given to you is that the spirit of God does reside within you. It is the spirit of God that gives you the ability to be everlasting and immortal. For truly, since you are the child of our Creator, in reality, you are also God, a part of God.

Just as God gave you the power to create, you also have the power to heal yourself through the spirit of God that resides within you. You have the ability not only to heal yourself spiritually, but also to heal yourself physically. You have the ability to forgive yourself for all of your past acts that may have caused pain or harm to others, for God embraces you totally in providing you forgiveness and love, for you are God's loving child. As God has created the earth as well as our universe, surely God has given you power, wisdom and strength to also create in yourself the ability to be at one with God, in spirit as well as in mind.

As we all journey through life, there are many things that we have done that have caused us to have remorse.

These may have included words or actions that we later recognize have caused hurt or damage to some of our brothers and sisters. We truly ask, dear God, that we are able to wipe the marks that have been caused by these actions from our soul. These marks have been an expression by us of something other than love or compassion for our brothers and sisters.

If there ever has been a time in your life when you expressed anger, and, in so doing, hurt another and you realize today that you should not have done so, now is the time to forgive yourself. God forgives you, Jeshua forgives you, and your angels forgive you. You are now forgiven.

If there ever has been a time in your life when you took advantage of another, and you knew it was wrong, now is the time to remove that mark from your soul, as you proceed in purifying your soul. God forgives you, Jeshua forgives you, and your angels forgive you. You are forgiven.

If there has ever been a time in your life that you criticized another, and in so doing, you caused that person hurt or pain, now is the time to forgive yourself. God forgives you, Jeshua forgives you, and your angels forgive you. You are forgiven.

If there was ever a time in your life when you showed a lack of patience toward another, and in so doing, you created a scar on your soul, for you hurt that individual as a result of your impatience, you now may forgive yourself. God forgives you, Jeshua forgives you, and your angels forgive you. You are forgiven.

If there was ever a time in your life you committed an act of selfishness toward another, and in doing so, hurt that other individual, now is the time to forgive yourself. God forgives you, Jeshua forgives you, and your angels forgive you. You are forgiven.

If there ever has been a time in your life when you were rude to another, and in that rudeness you caused another pain, now is the time to forgive yourself. The Lord forgives you, your loving brother Jeshua forgives you, and your angels forgive you. You are now forgiven.

If there ever has been a time in your life when you have shown prejudice toward another, and in so doing, hurt that brother or sister, now is the time to forgive yourself. Now is the time to remove that mark from your soul. God forgives you, Jeshua forgives you, and your angels forgive you. You are forgiven.

If there ever has been a time in your life when you lied to another, and in that lie you brought pain and heartache to that person, now is the time to forgive yourself. God forgives you, Jeshua forgives you, and your loving angels forgive you. You are forgiven.

If there ever has been a time in your life that another has asked you for your generosity, and you chose not to give it to that person and it left a scar on your soul, now is the time to forgive yourself. God forgives you, Jeshua forgives you, and your angels forgive you. And you are now forgiven.

If there ever has been a time in your life that someone has done something for you, and you showed a lack of gratitude and this has left a hurt on your soul because you knew this was not right, you may forgive yourself now. God forgives you, Jeshua forgives you, and your loving angels forgive you. You are forgiven.

If there ever was a time in your life that a person put out a hand in friendship to you, but you chose not to extend friendship and you have remorse and sadness within you for not having done so, now is the time to forgive yourself. The Lord forgives you, your brother Jeshua forgives you, and the angels forgive you. And you are now forgiven.

If there ever has been a time in your life when you have deceived another for your own benefit, and you knew it was wrong, and it left a mark on your soul, forgive yourself. God forgives you, Jeshua forgives you, and your loving angels forgive you. You are now forgiven.

If there has ever been a time in your life that you showed fear when you should have shown courage and it left a sadness in your heart and a scar on your soul, now is the time to forgive yourself. The Lord forgives you, your brother Jeshua forgives you, and the angels forgive you. You are forgiven.

If there ever was a time in your life when you were motivated by greed, and in so being, this false value created a hardship for another, now is the time to forgive yourself. God forgives you, Jeshua forgives you, and the angels forgive you. You are now forgiven.

Bring back the memory of any act that you have performed in your life that has caused pain or anguish to another, that created a mark on your soul, that still exists. God has now given you permission, Jeshua has given you permission, and your angels have given you permission to forgive yourself for every such thought and every such act. You are totally cleansing your entire soul, so that your spirit is growing closer and closer to being at one with God. For you truly are a loving child of God, and God wants you to forgive yourself and start over.

Now that the gates to your heart and soul are open, it is also time to release all that is negatively affecting your soul. You are now releasing all the anger that is inside of you, regardless of its cause. You are releasing any hatred that you have inside of your heart and soul, regardless of its cause. You are releasing all negative feelings that are stored within you, that are poison to your heart and soul. You are releasing them now, as well as forever. They are no longer a part of you emotionally, for you shall, instead, from this day on, treat them intellectually.

Your dear beloved creator, God, your dear beloved brother, Jeshua, and all of your angels applaud you, sing praise to you and are proud of you. For you are releasing all that is negative that is within your temple of God, so that your heart and soul shall be totally pure and will contain only loving thoughts and loving feelings.

You have now cleansed every mark that is on your soul, so that your soul is fresh with the spirit of God. You have now released all negative things that were within your heart and soul, so that your soul now only contains those thoughts and emotions that are loving and caring. And now you are making a commitment to God, that you will live your life from this day on, according to "God's will." You are totally recognizing the need for you to embrace the laws of God, living your life in universal love, universal compassion, and truth. And in that recognition, your commitment is pure and is genuine. You are pledging from this moment on that you shall live your life totally committed to God's will in sharing with others universal love, universal compassion, and living in truth.

If, in opening up the gates to your heart and soul and having released all that which is negative and not part of God's will, and if, in having forgiven yourself for all those things that you know had left a mark on your soul and had caused you pain, because of the pain or heartache that you may have caused others, if in having done all of this, it has brought tears of joy to you, now is the time to release them. Now is the time to allow those tears to flow, as you have purged your soul and your spirit, your temple of God, from all that is in conflict with God's will, and you have now purified that which is inside of you that is a part of God. Allow the tears to flow if they are there, for you have performed a miracle unto yourself with the help of God, with the help of Jeshua, and with the help of your beloved angels. Please take a few minutes to reflect in these thoughts, by quieting your heart, your mind, and your soul and allow them to be at one with God.

We have embraced God's will together, as loving brothers and sisters, just as we know God wants us to do. We thank our beloved brother Jeshua for being an example on earth and showing us the way. And we thank you, those who are the messengers of God, our loving angels, for providing us protection and help from the moment that we were born onto this earth, and as we have traveled on our journeys through the years of our life.

I now want to share with you, my brothers and sisters, a prayer that has been given to me by "spirit," and I encourage you to repeat this prayer on a daily basis. This is a prayer that we should say together, at 4:44 in the afternoon, when we together create God's wave, which I shall share with you in the next chapter.

The Prayer

Dear God, we acknowledge that you are our creator, our Father and our Mother, and we love you and are grateful for the gifts you have given to us. We are honored that you blessed us with immortality by anointing us with your spirit.

Jeshua, we acknowledge you as our Lord's beloved Son, our Brother, and as our spiritual guide. We love you and are grateful for the example that you provided us through your life while on earth.

Our loving angel guides, we acknowledge that you are the Messengers of God who watch over us, protecting us, and inspiring us.

We ask you our Dear Lord, Jeshua, and our angels, in your unbounded mercy, that you forgive us who are your loving children, for our past failures to think, speak, and act according to your will. We repent for every word and every deed that has given pain to others. We ask you, with all our heart and our strength in total humility, to cleanse our spirits and our souls with your love and your light.

We humbly ask that you accept our commitment to live our lives, from this moment on, in accordance with your laws, embracing universal love, universal compassion, and living in truth.

We thank you, Lord, for healing all of our spiritual wounds, and we shall always remain faithful in our commitment to you from this moment on.

AMEN

Chapter
- 17 -
God's Wave

In 1997, Princess Diana of Great Britain died in a car accident in Paris, France. Had you been to London three weeks before her death and had asked the people of London how they felt about Diana, some would have told you that she was a "playgirl," running around with the wrong crowd; others would have told you that she was an opportunist; and others would have said that she had been overexposed, was a publicity hound.

But when Princess Diana died, a spiritual consciousness began in the city of London that spread across the entire United Kingdom and then continued to spread across the world. Two billion people mourned her death. They remembered her for the good things she had done in her life, for her charity, and for her compassion.

Yes, there is a spiritual consciousness that truly is spreading around the entire world today, like never before in the history of mankind. Yes, people's minds are opening their gates, and information is being allowed to come into the hearts and souls of people in greater abundance than ever before in the history of our world.

It only takes a small percentage of the population of the world to create spiritual consciousness. Just as it first began in London with the death of Princess Diana, together we can create a wave of spiritual consciousness, a wave that is so powerful that it is filled with the love and energy of God, Jeshua, and all of our angels and guides from the spiritual world. That wave will grow larger and stronger and soon will be part of everything that is around us, the air that we breath and the energy that surrounds us and our globe.

Let us agree that at 4:44 on Sunday afternoon on the 4th of April, 1999, this wave of spiritual consciousness shall begin in the time zone of the eastern part of the United States. Those of you who are able to travel, come join us at the Lincoln Memorial in Washington D.C., which is the capitol of our country. Our ceremonies will begin several hours earlier, and at 4:44 in the afternoon eastern time, we shall all pray together. We shall create a wave of spiritual consciousness that will spread throughout the entire world, from time zone to time zone.

Let thousands of us gather together at the Lincoln Memorial and create God's wave. As that wave of energy and love spreads westward, our brothers and sisters in the next time zone and in each time zone thereafter, at 4:44 in the afternoon on the fourth day of the fourth month, will join us in this wave of spiritual consciousness; this wave containing God's love and energy, until it reaches the western shores of our continent, then crosses the Pacific Ocean and westward across the entire globe.

And in every country, every province, every state, every city, every town, let leaders step forward who will help organize their brothers and sisters and encourage and recruit and convince all of our brothers and sisters to join us, to be a part of that spiritual consciousness.

This energy and love will be felt all over the world. It will rise and ring throughout the heavens. It will affect the hearts and souls of people of every society, in every corner of the world. And God, Jeshua, Siddhartha, Mohammed, Maya Babar, and all the great avatars, and all the light beings and angels in the spirit world, and all our brothers and sisters who are now living in the spirit world will rejoice, applaud, and celebrate the commitment we have made, the commitment as a people of the world, who together are committed to embracing universal love, universal compassion, and living in truth.

We shall continue this spiritual consciousness on the fourth Sunday of every month thereafter at 4:44 in the afternoon, in every country, province, state, city, and town. We will continue our prayers and allow the wave of spiritual consciousness that we have created to grow and grow, until we have become one with our commitment to God, until we, indeed, make it on earth as it is in heaven.

You can step forward and be a messenger. Help organize your brothers and sisters in your own communities and cities. Select locations for people to gather in each city and town. Visit the local churches, clubs, and associations. Speak on your local radio and television stations. Gather together in communities and organize. We will share with you the details of this glorious day that will begin on Sunday, April 4, 1999, and continue on the fourth Sunday of every month at 4:44 P.M. thereafter. We shall provide you updated information in our monthly newsletter.

Together we shall bring in the new millennium. We shall commit ourselves to God's will and we shall live our lives embracing universal love, universal compassion, and living in truth.

The Great Tomorrow

We encourage you to write to us. Share with us your thoughts, "444" experiences, and comments about *In God's Truth*. We also want to know if you are willing to be a part of God's spiritual wave scheduled for the 4th of April, 1999.

Because of the overwhelming response we have received from our readers, we created a monthly newsletter which includes events that are taking place surrounding the continued work of Nick Bunick and his colleagues, including healings, human interest stories, notable "444" experiences happening to many people who have read *The Messengers*, as well as dates for symposiums that we will be having around the country.

If you would like to receive our newsletter, we are hopeful you are able to make a voluntary contribution of $20.00, representing twelve monthly issues, in order to cover the expenses and defray costs of our nonprofit corporation. If you cannot afford to make a donation, we will still place your name on our mailing list, and perhaps those who can afford a larger donation, would assist in helping those who cannot afford to contribute. Donations should be made out to The Great Tomorrow, and any excess income will be used for spiritual and humanitarian projects.

If you are interested in owning a copy of the reproduction of the portrait of Jeshua, you may also contact us at the address below. The reproduction of Jeshua, including handling and shipping charges, is $29.00 per copy in the United States and Canada. For all other international orders, an additional charge of $20.00 for shipping and handling should be included with your payment.

Our mailing address for correspondence and to order the newsletter or the portrait of Jeshua is:

The Great Tomorrow
P.O. Box 2222
Lake Oswego, OR 97035

Our e-mail address is TGT444@aol.com. Our website address is fourfourfour.com.

God bless you as you continue on your journey.

The Great Tomorrow